MW01691146

Social Studies Alive!®

Our Community and Beyond

Student Journal

Welcome to your *Social Studies Alive!* Student Journal

This journal is your place to read, reflect, and create. It works hand in hand with your online access.

In each lesson, you'll find:

- Preview Activity
- Vocabulary Activity
- Hands-On Activity
- Reading
- Show What You Know

In addition, look for the Activity Online callouts throughout the journal. These indicate that additional activity directions and interactions are online.

Every lesson also includes opportunities to dive deeper online, including:

- Lesson Games
- Vocabulary Cards
- Slideshows
- Videos and songs
- Primary Sources and more!

Sign in at **www.teachtci.com** to see all resources.

TCi™

CONTENTS

Unit 1 Geography 1

Create a three-dimensional model of Earth to demonstrate your geography skills. Build and use a compass to locate U.S. landmarks. Design a brochure that illustrates the geography of your community. Find hidden objects that reveal how Native Americans interacted with their environments. Conduct an inquiry to explain what Liberty State Park reveals about how humans interact with geography.

Unit 2 History

Analyze primary sources to explore immigration throughout U.S. history. Study the characteristics of culture and play a game themed on your community. Honor a citizen-leader who improved their community. Travel to other countries to learn about their cultures. Conduct an inquiry to investigate how history and culture influence your community.

Unit 3 Economics 195

Bring economic images to life and then ask your own questions about the economy. Experience being a buyer and seller in a marketplace. Debate real-life economic situations and play a game to test your budgeting skills. Take on the role of countries conducting trade around the world. Conduct an inquiry to explore the role of scarcity in the world around us.

Unit 4 Civics 273

Explore different community services and rank their importance. Plan and write a podcast about government. Bring to life important steps in being a good citizen, such as speaking at a public meeting. Plan and carry out a service project to make a difference in the world. Conduct an inquiry to find out why it is important to be a good citizen.

A Whole New Way to Experience Social Studies

Inquiry-Based Unit Structures
Each unit starts with an intriguing storyline and compelling question that piques students' interest and drives instruction throughout the lesson. They are encouraged to draw upon and apply previous knowledge and also use outside resources and Social Studies Stories to expand their answer.

Student-Centered Activities
Each lesson utilizes at least one of TCI's unique, hands-on strategies to get students thinking, moving, and asking big questions. Students are inspired to learn more and engage in fun activities, which they can access both online and in the Journal.

Culturally-Responsive Content
Meaningful standards-aligned content with opportunities for making personal connections and participating in an inclusive classroom environment.

Online Resources
Ready-to-teach presentations, activities, complete student resources, customizable assessments and more at your fingertips!

Unit 1

Geography

Create a three-dimensional model of Earth to demonstrate your geography skills. Build and use a compass to locate U.S. landmarks. Design a brochure that illustrates the geography of your community. Find hidden objects that reveal how Native Americans interacted with their environments. Conduct an inquiry to explain what Liberty State Park reveals about how humans interact with geography.

Unit Inquiry Project

1 Gathering Visual Evidence

List five interesting details you see in this photograph.	
Where do you think this might be? What clues could help you figure it out?	
Why might there be rusted metal and other trash in this image?	

2 Developing the Compelling Question

Unit Storyline

This photograph was taken in New Jersey. You're looking at the back side of a famous U.S. monument, the Statue of Liberty. The photo was taken in the 1970s, when this area was an abandoned railroad yard. Today, Liberty State Park is here, and it looks very different!

Unit Compelling Question

How does Liberty State Park relate to geography and how humans interact with geography?

List three questions you have about the Unit Storyline and Compelling Question.

1.

2.

3.

3 Collecting Evidence

After you complete each lesson, return to this table and answer the questions. You will be gathering key information that will help you complete the Unit Inquiry Project.

Lesson	Supporting Questions	What I Learned
1 Understanding the Geography of the World	The photograph was taken in New Jersey. In which country, continent, and hemisphere is New Jersey located? Where is your community?	
2 Finding Places in the United States	What famous landmark did you learn about that you see in the image? What landmarks are in your community?	
3 Geography and the Way We Live	Where do you see natural resources in the photograph? Where do you see pollution? How does geography affect life in your community?	
4 Native Americans and Their Environments	How could you find out which Native Americans lived in New Jersey before Europeans arrived? How might they have interacted with their environment?	

4 Building Additional Content Knowledge

Gather and evaluate additional sources to answer the Unit Compelling Question: *How does Liberty State Park relate to geography and how we interact with it?*

Research Liberty State Park in New Jersey. Find out when it was built and why. Find out what it looks like today.

You may conduct outside research or use these readings from *Social Studies Alive! Our Community and Beyond* Social Studies Stories:

- Telling Stories with Maps
- One Immigrant's Story
- Finding New Sources of Energy
- Learning About Others Through Art

Source Title(s)	
Additional Evidence	

5 Constructing an Argument

Write a sentence answering the Unit Compelling Question: *How does Liberty State Park relate to geography and how we interact with it?* This is called a claim.

Then provide at least two pieces of evidence to support your claim. Your evidence can come from the activities you did in class, the readings you completed in your Student Journal or Social Studies Stories, or additional research that you conducted.

Claim:

Evidence:

6 Taking Informed Action

Decide how you want to share what you learned. You could make a poster, a digital presentation, or a video. You might share your presentation with your classmates or with adults in the community.

Lesson 1

Understanding the Geography of the World

Where in the world is our community?

Introduction

Picture yourself as an astronaut in a spacecraft. If you looked at the planet Earth from space, what do you think you would see? Maybe clouds, land, and water? What would you need to know to find your landing site on Earth?

To answer these questions, you need to know some geography. Geography is the study of Earth—its land, water, air, and people. In this lesson, you will learn about how Earth can be divided into different pieces.

You will come across important geography vocabulary words, such as *hemispheres*, *continents*, *countries*, and *states*. These words describe pieces that make up Earth. They will also help you use maps to find any place on Earth—from space or from your classroom.

Vocabulary

border
capital
continent
country
equator
geography
government
ocean
prime meridian
state

From space, you can see much of Earth. Where on Earth do you live?

Preview Activity

Activity Online

Draw a map of the location of your desk in the classroom.

Vocabulary Activity

Activity Online

Label each image with terms from its word bank.

Vocabulary Word Bank

- continent
- equator
- ocean
- prime meridian

Oceans and Continents

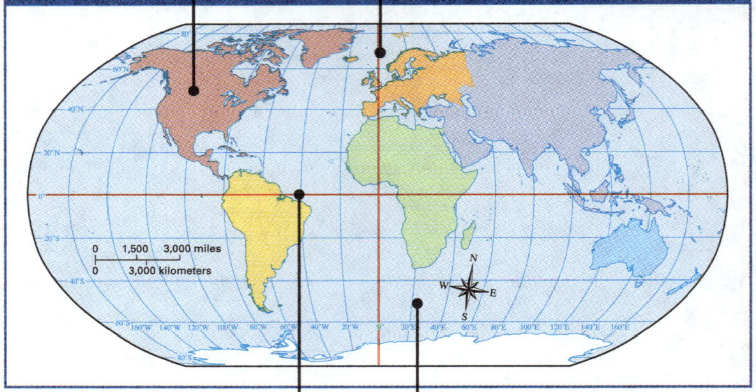

Vocabulary Word Bank

- border
- capital
- country
- geography
- state

United States Political Map

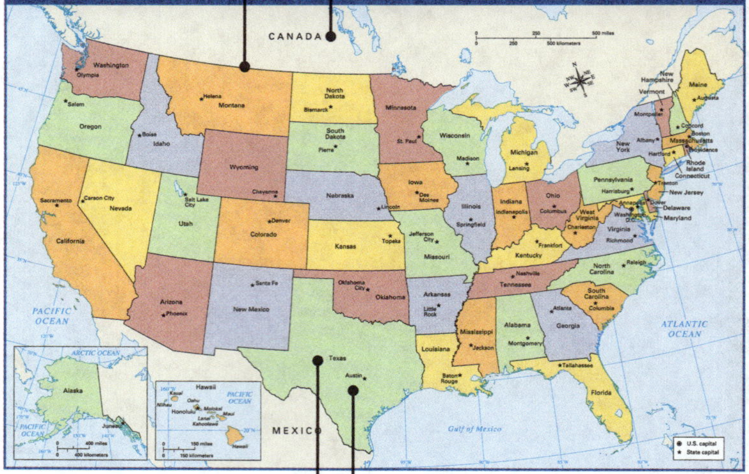

________________________ is the study of Earth—its spaces, land, water, air, and people.

Hands-On Activity

Create a three-dimensional model of Earth. Then use it to answer a series of geography questions.

Directions: Modeling Earth

1. **Read Sections 1–5.** Learn about important geography terms and how to find places on maps.
2. **Complete the maps in your Activity Notes.** Follow the directions to label the map of the world and the map of the United States.
3. **Get into pairs and gather materials.** Make sure you have a balloon, marker, scissors, and glue. You will also need the two Activity Cutouts pages in this journal with the continents and oceans.
4. **Build your balloon globe.** Follow the directions in your Activity Notes. Label the equator, prime meridian, and hemispheres. Add the continents and compass rose. Label the continents and oceans.
5. **Use your balloon globe to answer questions about Earth!**

1. Our Community Is on Planet Earth

You can only see half of Earth at a time. Half of a sphere is known as a hemisphere.

Remember that you are an astronaut in outer space. From your spacecraft, you can see how big Earth looks outside your window. You will see clouds, water, and land. You may also see mountains, deserts, and other things on Earth. These are all part of Earth's **geography**.

How would you describe the shape of Earth? Earth is not flat. Instead, you may notice that Earth is shaped like a ball. What else is shaped like a ball? Another word for an object shaped like a ball is a sphere. If you cut a sphere in half, you get two hemispheres. Hemisphere means half of a sphere. Earth is broken up into several hemispheres.

Imagine a line around the middle of Earth, like a belt that goes around your waist. Many maps of Earth have a line like this called the **equator**. The equator divides Earth into the Northern Hemisphere and the Southern Hemisphere.

You can also divide a sphere from top to bottom. Imagine a line that starts at the top of Earth at the North Pole and runs down one side of Earth to the bottom at the South Pole. There is a special line like this on maps of Earth. It passes through the city of Greenwich, in England. We call this line the **prime meridian**. It divides Earth into the Western Hemisphere and the Eastern Hemisphere.

Find the equator and the prime meridian on the maps. How many hemispheres do you see?

Hemispheres

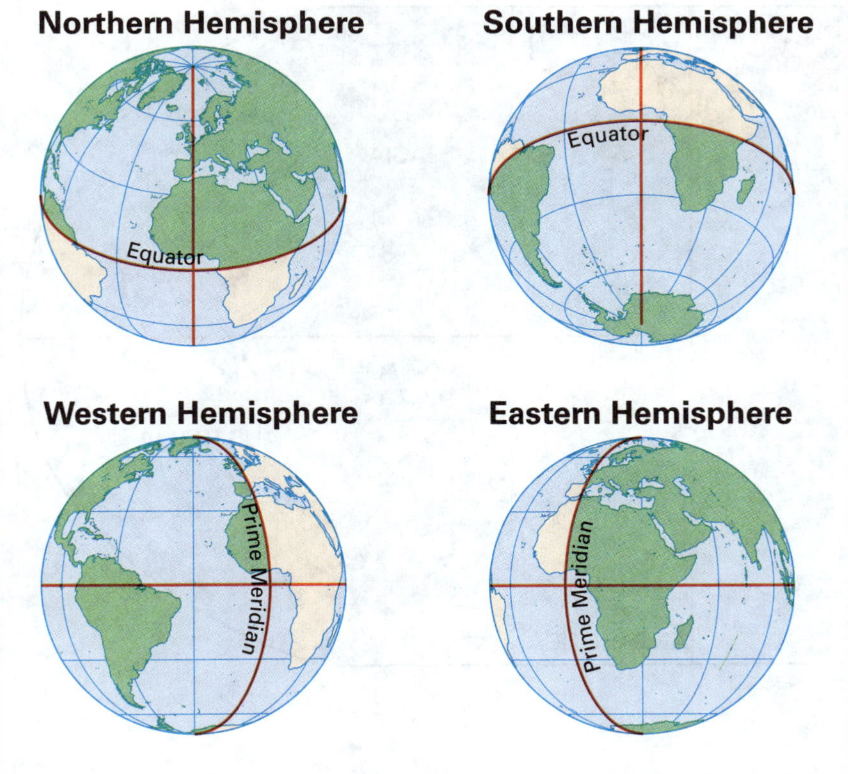

The equator separates the Northern and Southern hemispheres, while the prime meridian divides the Western and Eastern hemispheres. Which hemispheres are you a part of?

2. Our Community Is on a Continent

From space, you can see that most of Earth is covered with water. The largest bodies of water are called **oceans**.

There are five oceans on Earth. They are called the Pacific Ocean, the Atlantic Ocean, the Indian Ocean, the Southern Ocean, and the Arctic Ocean. Look at the map to find the five oceans.

The oceans wrap around large bodies of land. These areas of land are called **continents**.

There are seven continents on Earth. They are called Africa, Antarctica, Asia, Australia, Europe, North America, and South America.

Earth consists of land and sea. The land is divided into continents, and the sea is divided into oceans.

Oceans and Continents

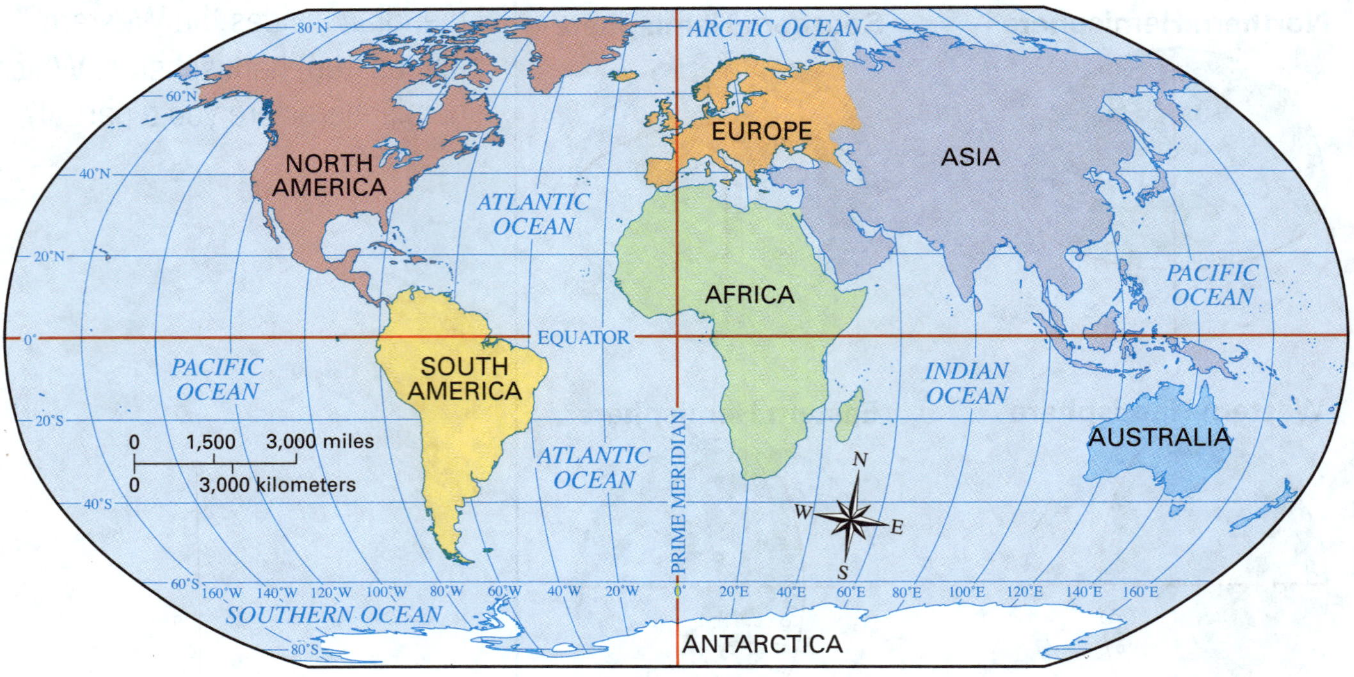

Asia is the largest continent, and Australia is the smallest. You can look at a map to find each of the seven continents. You can see that each continent has a different color on the *Oceans and Continents* map.

Each continent also has its own shape. The continents are mostly surrounded by oceans, but many of them are connected to each other by land in certain places.

On which continent do you live? Do you live near an ocean?

Each of the seven continents looks different. Which continent is this?

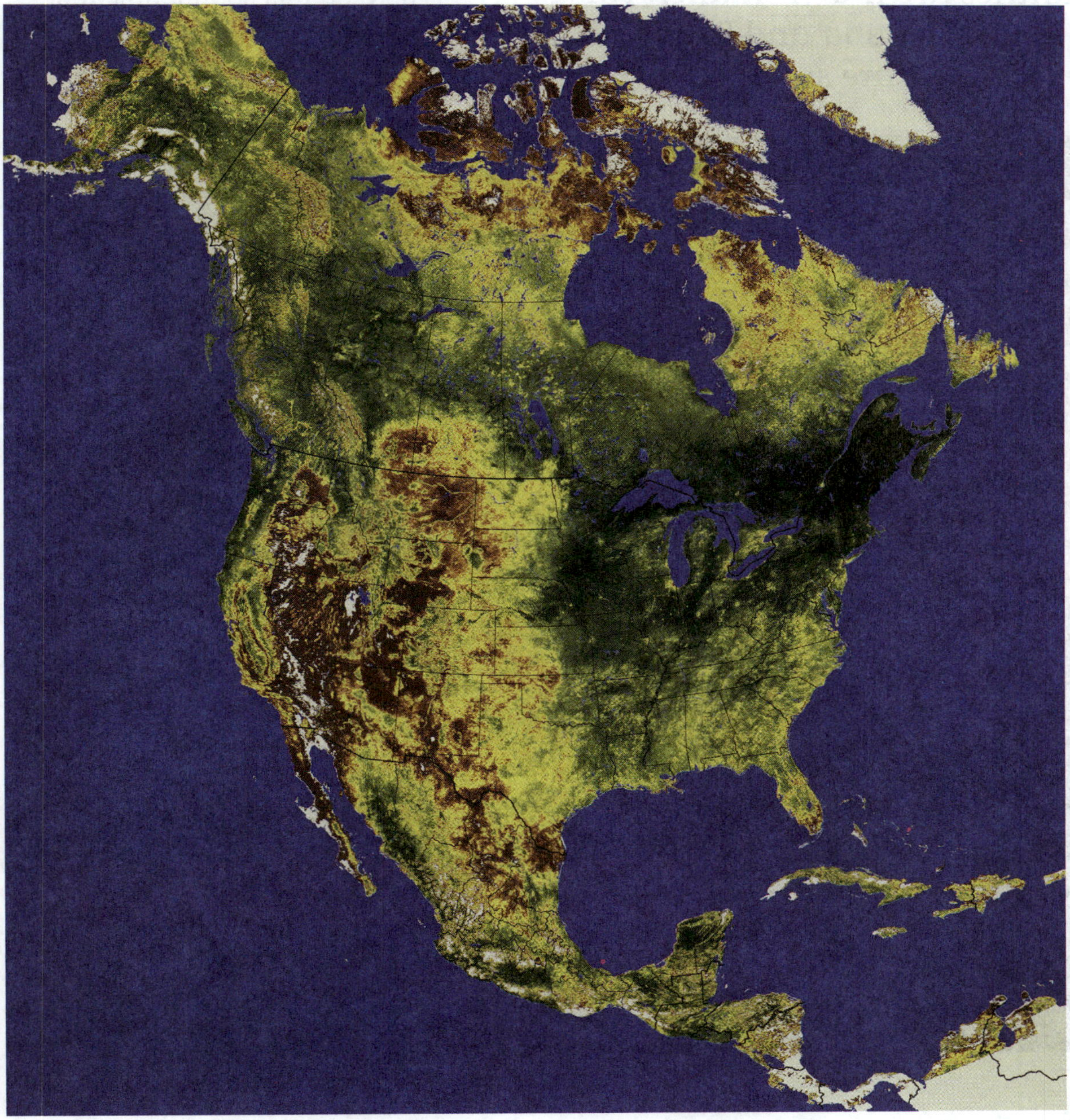

3. Our Community Is in a Country

Now you are steering the spacecraft toward your continent. Can you land just anywhere? What part of the continent do you need to find? Most continents have many **countries**. A country is an area of land that has its own **government**.

Some countries are very large. For example, if you look at Canada and the United States on a map, you will see that they are quite large.

Other countries are much smaller. For example, if you find Cuba and El Salvador, you will see that they are small countries.

Where on this continent is the country that you are going to land your spacecraft?

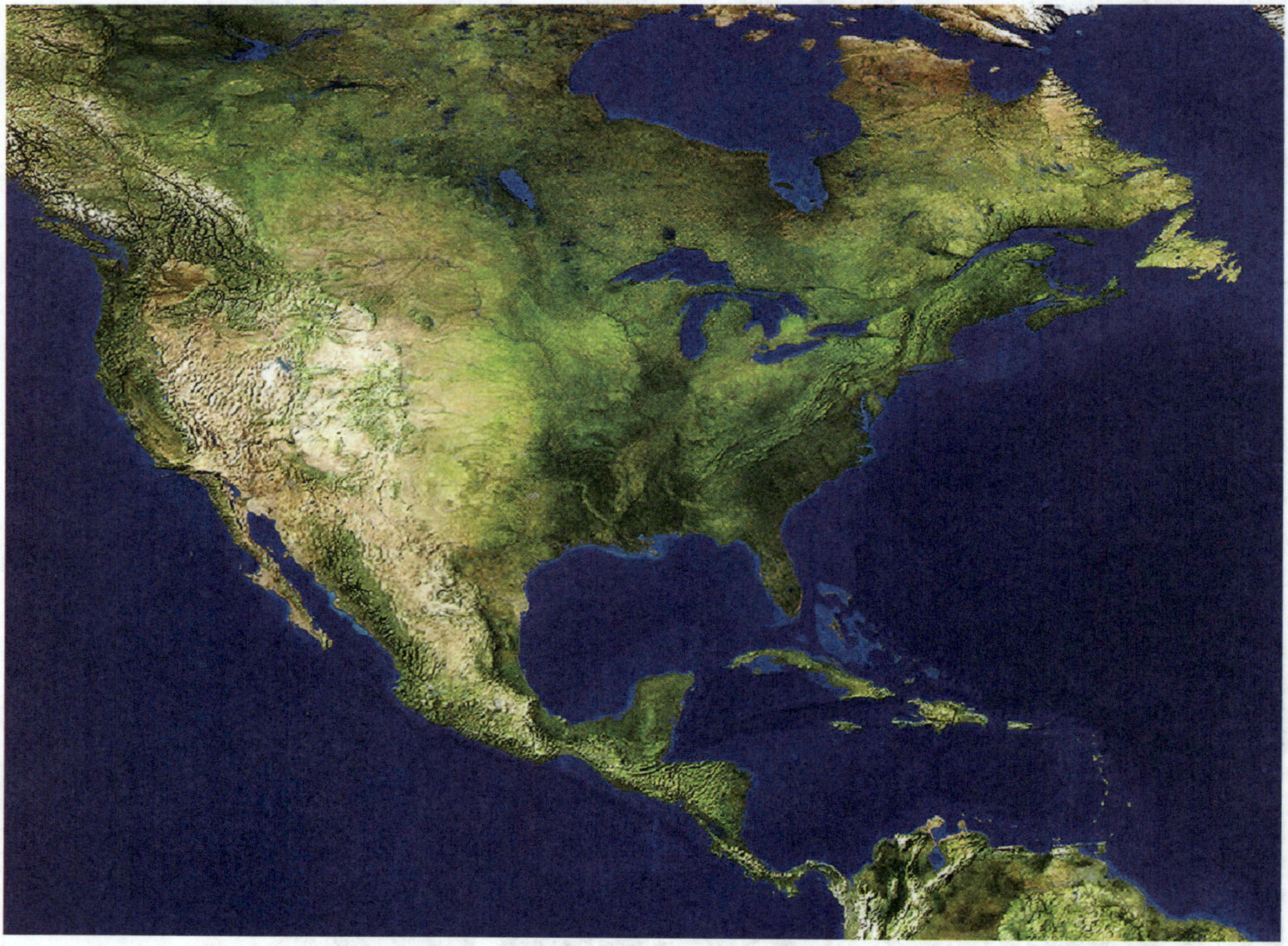

Every country has **borders** that surround it. A border is the line where one place, such as a country, ends and another begins. From space, you cannot see all borders. On a map, you can see lines drawn around each country to show its borders. Sometimes mountains, rivers, and oceans help to make borders. At other times, countries have to agree on where their borders will be.

How many countries can you find on the map? Where is your country on the map?

These are the countries of North America. Which of them do you live in?

Countries in North America

4. Our Community Is in a State

The spacecraft is zooming toward the United States. The United States is a big country. How will you find the landing spot?

Most large countries are divided into many smaller parts. In the United States, these smaller parts are called **states**. These states share many similarities, but each of these states is unique.

Each state has its own government. Each state has a flag and state motto. Suppose you are in Texas. If you looked around, you would probably find the Texas flag waving. You would probably also find the United States flag. People are proud of living in their state, but they are also proud of living in their country.

Your landing spot is in the water near a certain state. Can you figure out which state the spacecraft is flying toward?

This image was taken with a satellite from space. Can you tell which of the 50 states it is showing?

Like countries, states in the United States have borders. However, you cannot see many borders of states from space.

Luckily, you have a map that shows part of the United States. Each state is a different color with borders surrounding it.

Some borders are natural. For example, look at Florida's border. Only part of Florida touches the land. The rest of it sticks out into the Atlantic Ocean and the Gulf of Mexico. Because of this, most of Florida's border is made by water.

Some borders must be agreed on between states. These borders are not natural. What states are next to Florida? Alabama and Georgia share a border with Florida.

Florida, like every state, has borders. Can you spot which of Florida's borders are natural and which had to be decided on?

Some U.S. States

5. Finding Communities in a State

Mission control confirms that you are headed for the state of Florida. States are made up of many communities. Communities are places where people live, work, and play. Each state has different types of communities.

Some communities are called cities. Cities are big communities with many tall buildings and people.

Look at the map of Florida. A map of a state will show places with the most people. These are usually cities. Tallahassee, Tampa, and Pensacola are cities in Florida.

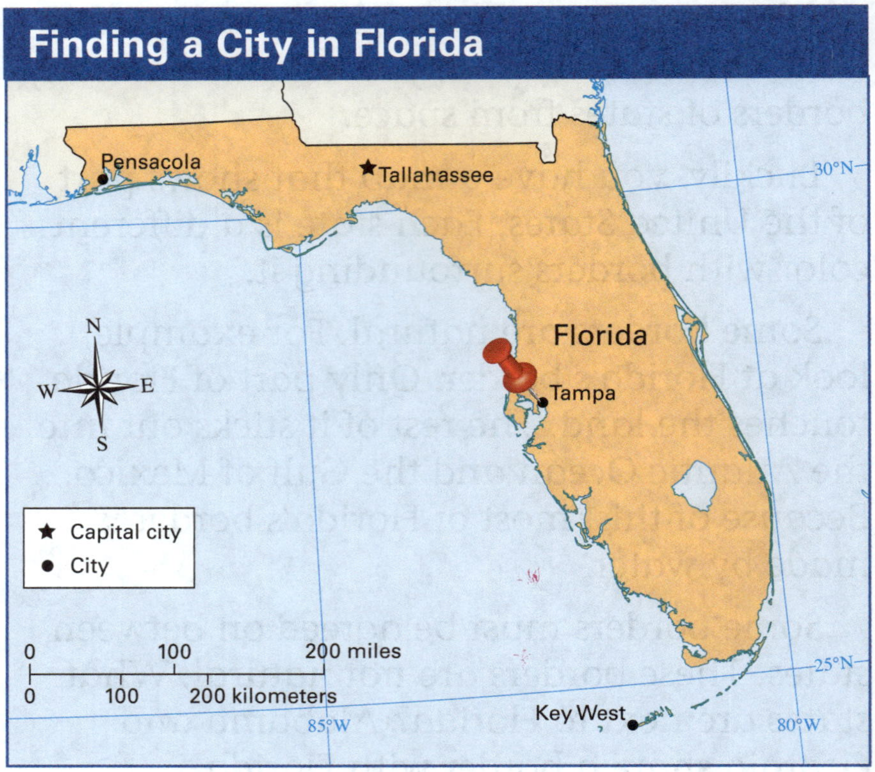

Tampa is one of the biggest cities in Florida.

Tallahassee is starred on the map, which means that it is the **capital** city. The government of Florida is in Tallahassee. Florida's laws are made there.

Cities are large communities, but other communities are smaller. They have fewer people than cities do. We call these communities towns.

Most of the map does not have any city names, but this does not mean there are no communities there. There are communities all over Florida. Some of them are smaller towns. For example, one of these towns is Micanopy. It is smaller than a large city like Tampa.

The community closest to where you are landing is Pensacola. Can you find it?

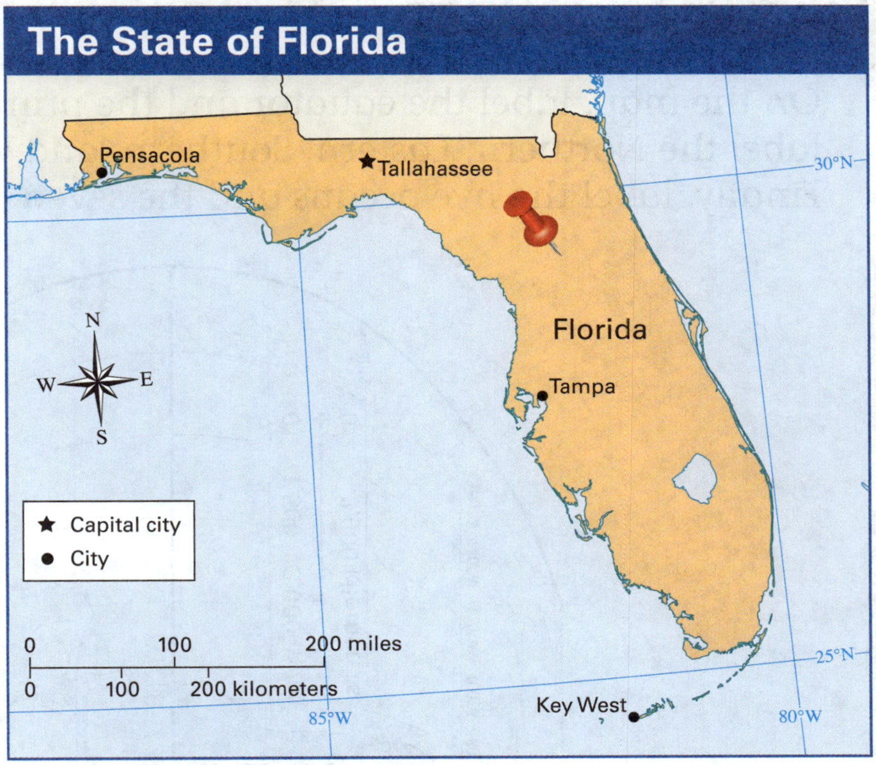

The pin on the map shows where the town of Micanopy is.

Hands-On Activity Notes

Activity Online

On the map, label the equator and the prime meridian. Then, label the Northern, Eastern, Southern, and Western hemispheres. Finally, label the five oceans and the seven continents.

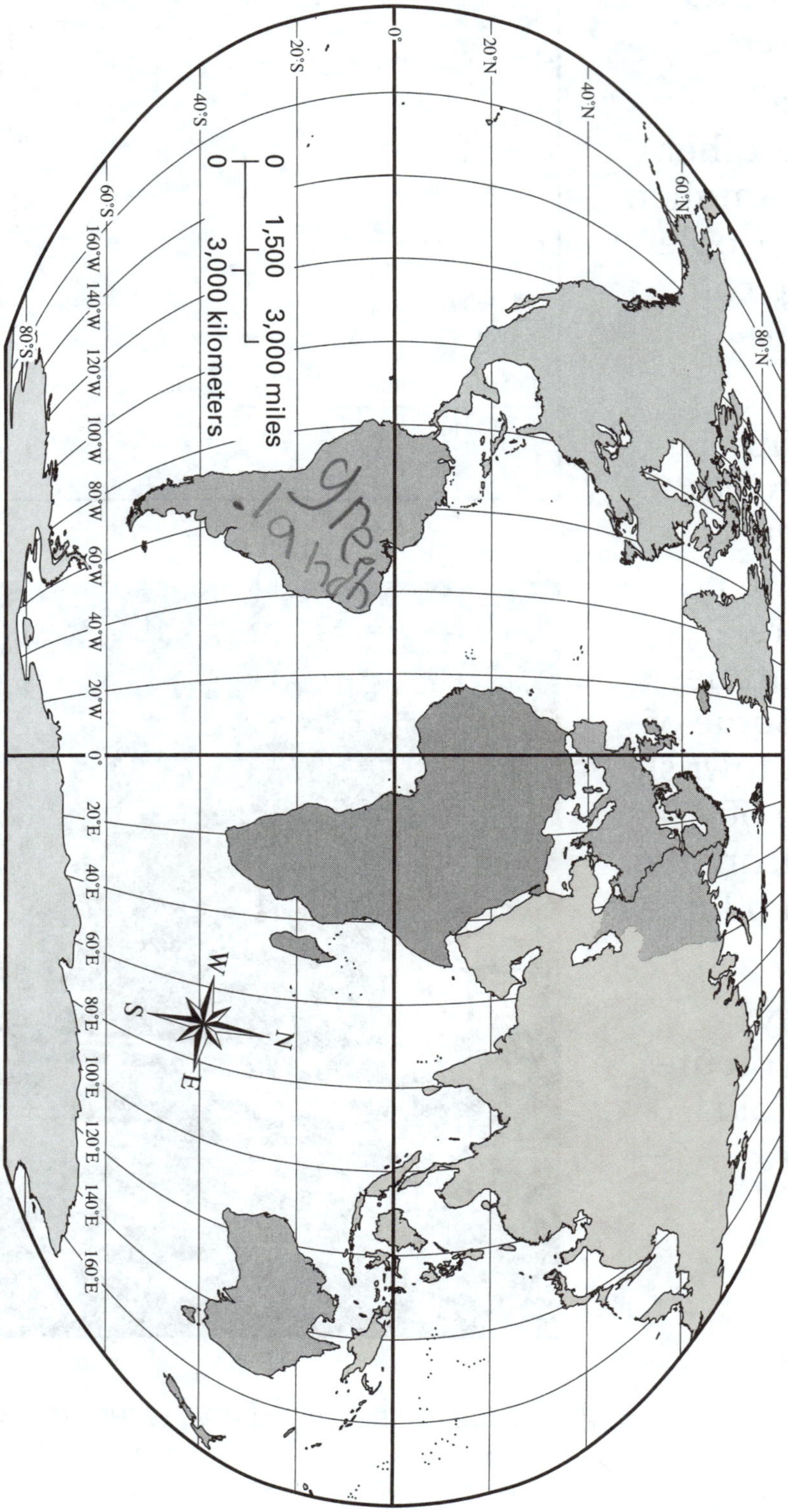

Label five countries on the map. Be sure to spell the names correctly. Then research where your state is located. Label it on the map.

Follow the directions to make and label your balloon globe.

1. Blow up your balloon.

- Make sure it has a round shape, but do not overfill it.
- Tie the end of your balloon so that no air escapes.

2. Label the equator, prime meridian, and hemispheres.

- With your partner, decide who will write on the balloon and who will hold the balloon.
- Use a marker to add the labels. Make sure to spell the names correctly.

3. Add the continents and compass rose.

- Cut out the continents and compass rose from your Activity Notes.
- Put glue on the backs of the continent cutouts and place them on your balloon globe. Think about their position and distance from one another.
- Glue on the compass rose where there is room. Make sure it is pointing in the right direction.

4. Label the continents and oceans.

- Cut out the labels from your Activity Notes.
- Put glue on the backs of the labels one at a time. Place your labels in the correct locations on your balloon globe.
- Repeat this for all continents and ocean labels.

5. Check to see that everything is properly labeled. Then get ready to use your model to answer geography questions.

Summary

In this lesson, you learned how to tell where places are on Earth using maps. The names of hemispheres, continents, countries, and states all help us to say where a place is located. Maps show borders of places. Some borders are made by mountains and rivers, but others are decided on by people.

The spacecraft you were on was headed toward a community in Florida. You saw the continent and country that Florida is part of, but you might live somewhere else. Where on Earth do you live?

Show What You Know

Create a map to show where your community is located. Follow these steps:

- On the line provided, write the name of your community.
- Conduct research, using print or online maps, to find out where your community is located.
- Draw a large outline of your state.
- Draw a dot in your state to show where your community is. If your community is the state capital, draw a star to show where your community is.

Flip the page →

Community: ______________________________

Lesson 2

Finding Places in the United States

Where in the United States is our community?

Introduction

What do you notice when you look at a map of the United States? You may notice the borders of states in the country. You may notice tools that help you find places on the map. Maps help you dream about places you want to visit.

What places would you want to visit in the United States? You might want to go see the Statue of Liberty or the Golden Gate Bridge. If you want to know how to get to these places, you can use a map. Maps can tell you how far a place is from your community. They can tell you which direction to go to get to the place.

You will learn how you can find your community on a map of the United States. You will read about some famous places in this country and where you can find them on a map. You can use maps to discover where these places are compared to your community.

Vocabulary

canyon
cardinal direction
map key
scale
symbol

This student is using a map to locate her community.

Preview Activity

Activity Online

Draw a simple map of your classroom and label it with these eight directions: north, northeast, east, southeast, south, southwest, west, and northwest.

Vocabulary Activity

Activity Online

Use the word bank to label the parts of this map.

Vocabulary Word Bank

canyon | cardinal direction | map key | scale | symbol

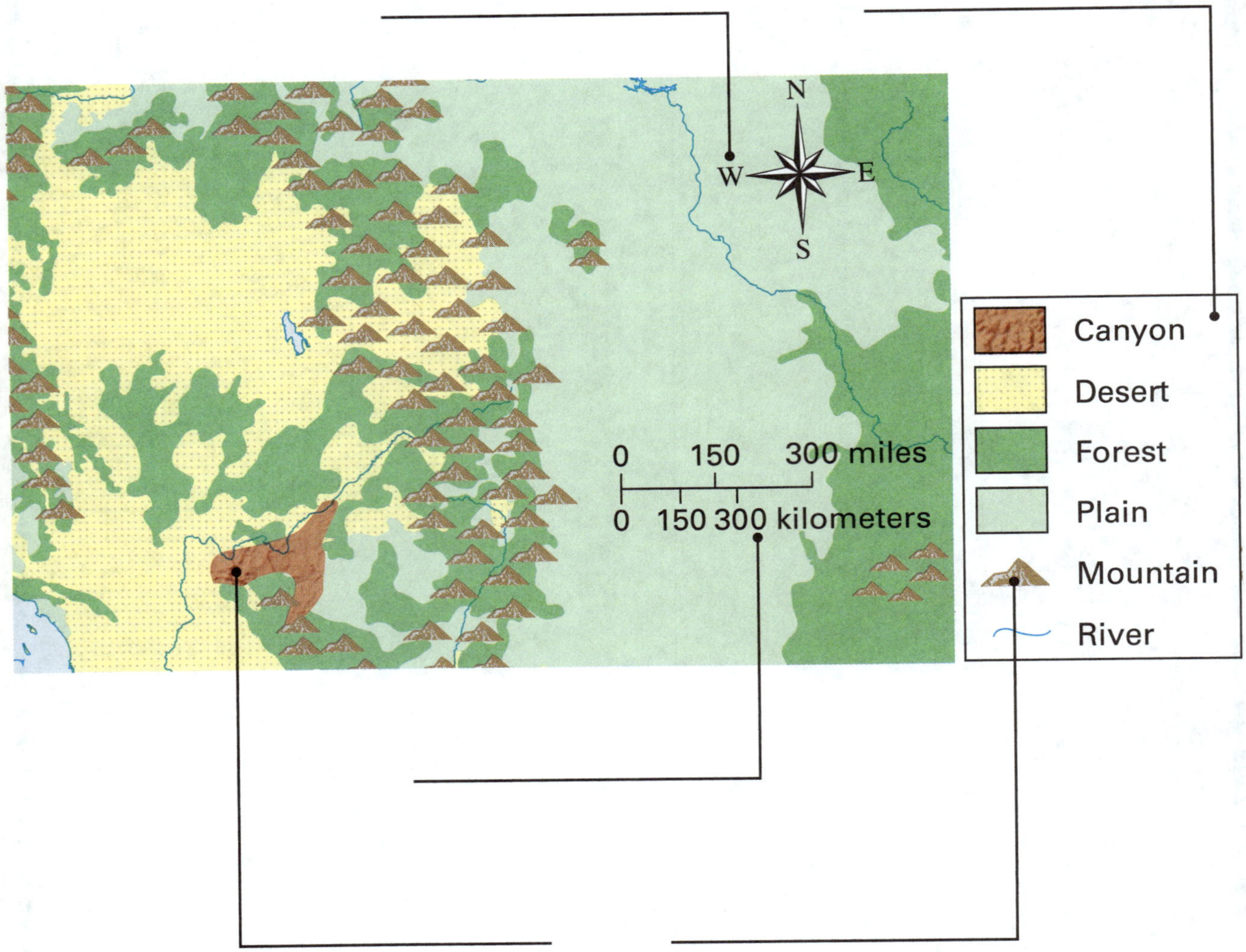

Hands-On Activity

Build a compass and use it to find the direction of six landmarks across the United States. Learn how to use map scales and estimate the distance from your community to famous U.S. landmarks.

Directions: Using a Compass

1. **Sit with your partner and notice the photographs around the room.** As you look out from the center of the United States you will see eight landmarks placed on the walls around your classroom.
2. **Assemble your compass and orient it to point north.** Cut out your compass and attach the blue pointer with a brad. Place it on your desk and make sure the arrow is pointing toward the "North" sign posted on your classroom wall.
3. **Use your compass and pointer to answer the questions.** Keep your compass oriented to the north and move the blue pointer around to point to the various landmarks.
4. **Debrief as a class.** Review the answers with your class. How did you do?
5. **Read Sections 1–8 and complete your Activity Notes.**

Directions: Scale Puzzles

1. **As a class, practice measuring the distance between two U.S. cities.**
2. **Complete your Activity Notes.** You will work on your own to estimate the distance between various locations you have mapped and labeled.
3. **Check your answers.**

Hands-On Activity Notes

Activity Online

Use your compass, compass pointer, and the photographs around your classroom to answer these questions as if you were standing in the geographical center of the continental United States.

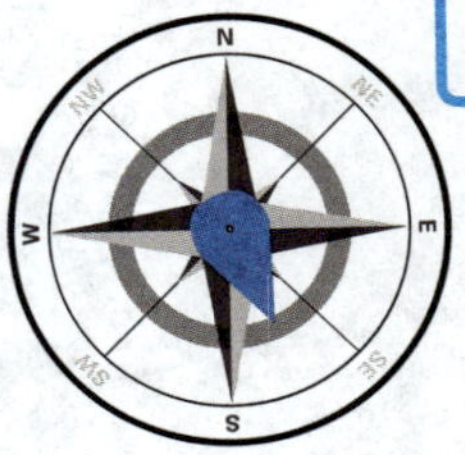

Question	Your Answer
1. "North" is an example of which type of direction?	
2. "Southeast" is an example of which type of direction?	
3. In which direction is the Grand Canyon?	
4. What do you see when you look directly to the south?	
5. What do you see when you look toward the northeast?	
6. In which direction is the Statue of Liberty?	
7. In which direction are the Everglades?	
8. What do you see when you look toward the northwest?	
9. In which direction is the Golden Gate Bridge?	
10. What do you see when you look directly north?	

1. The 50 States

When you write your address, you first write the name of your street and the name of your community. Then you write the name of your state. Your state is one of many in the United States.

The United States is the country where you live. It is a country in the continent of North America. The United States has 50 states. How many of them can you name? Which state would you like to visit?

Some states are well-known because they have famous places that people like to visit. Have you heard of the Grand Canyon? It is a famous place in the state of Arizona. The Statue of Liberty is a famous landmark in the state of New York.

When you write your address, you need to know which state you live in. There are 50 states in the United States.

The states are different from each other. The weather is warmer in some states and cooler in others. Some states are close to the ocean, and others are surrounded by land. In some states, you can see plenty of farmland, but in other states, you will find busy cities instead. How would you describe the state where you live?

Each state has communities in it. What is the name of the town or city where you live? This is your community. Some states have many communities with many people living in them, but other states have fewer communities that are located farther apart.

A community may have features or landmarks that make it different from other communities. What makes your community special?

The 50 states can be very different. Some states are close to the ocean, and others are surrounded by land.

2. Mapping the United States

You can use a map of the United States to find different states in the country.

Where is your state in the United States? Do you live close to or far from the ocean? Are you in the western or eastern part of the country? A map can help you answer these questions!

A map shows different places on Earth, including the United States. A map of the United States can show you the borders of the country and the 50 states.

You can figure out where your community is located in the United States by using a map. First, find the state you live in. Then, find the area where you live within the state.

Maps can also help you find other states in the country. Can you find New York, Florida, Illinois, South Dakota, Arizona, and California? You can compare their locations to your community's using the tools on a map.

Maps have a compass rose to show you the **cardinal directions,** which are north, east, south, and west. You can use the compass rose to find out if your state is to the east or west of the Mississippi River.

Maps also have **symbols**. The **map key** tells you what the symbols represent. For example, some maps have a star on them. The map key tells you that the star represents the U.S. capital.

A map's **scale** shows you distance. It can tell you how far places are from each other. On the map of the United States, you can use the scale to figure out how many miles South Dakota is from Arizona.

Now, you will learn about famous places in different states. You can use the map's tools to find out where they are located and how far away they are.

This map shows you where the 50 states are located.

Map of the United States

Hands-On Activity Notes

Activity Online

To complete the map, do the following:

- Label the compass rose, map key, and the scale.
- Find your state on the map and outline it.
- Draw a dot to mark your community in your state.

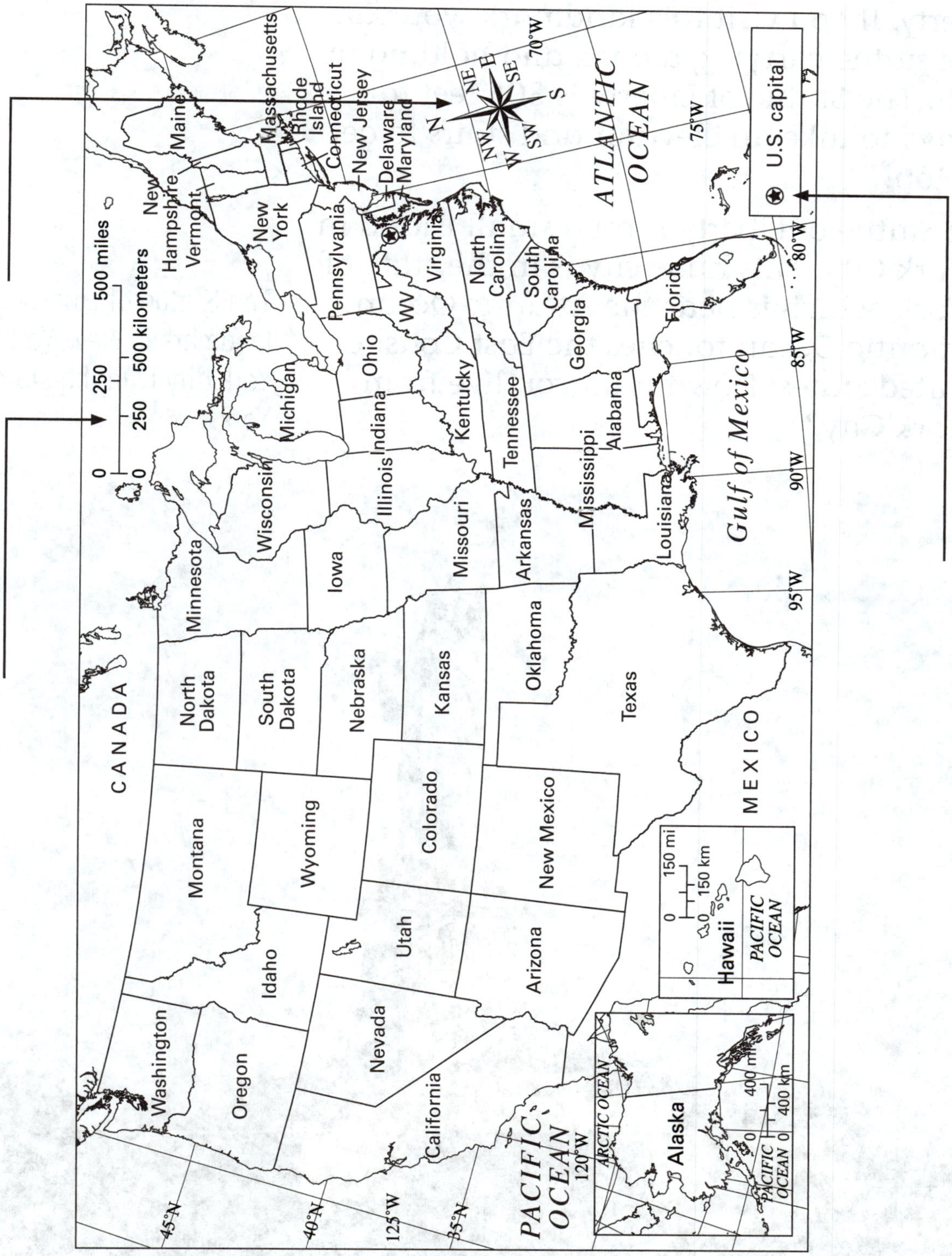

3. The Statue of Liberty

Do you recognize the statue in this image? This famous statue welcomes people to the United States. It stands for freedom. It is called the Statue of Liberty.

Every year, many people visit the Statue of Liberty. If you visit this landmark, you can see the statue carrying a book and holding up a torch. The Statue of Liberty is 305 feet tall. You have to take an elevator and stairs to get to the top!

The Statue of Liberty is on a small island in New York City. This huge city is in the state of New York, which is near the Atlantic Ocean. The Atlantic Ocean touches the East Coast of the United States. How far do you live from New York City?

The Statue of Liberty is a famous landmark in New York City. New York City is in the state of New York.

This alligator lives in the Everglades. The Everglades are a warm and wet area in the state of Florida.

4. The Everglades

Have you ever seen an alligator? Would you like to meet a crocodile? You can find these and other animals in a famous place called the Everglades.

The Everglades are warm and wet. If you visit the Everglades, you will notice that the land is soggy with tall grass growing out of it. Lots of birds, snakes, crocodiles, and alligators live there, too. People visit the Everglades to camp, to see wildlife, and to fish.

The Everglades are in the state of Florida. They cover a lot of land in the southern part of this state. Florida is north and east of the Gulf of Mexico. Do you live north or south of the Everglades?

5. The Willis Tower

The Willis Tower is the tallest building in this image. It is in Chicago, the biggest city in Illinois.

Many people work and live in downtown Chicago. It is a busy place with many tall buildings. Can you spot the tallest one?

The tallest building in Chicago is the Willis Tower. In fact, at 1,450 feet high, it is one of the tallest buildings in the world!

The Willis Tower opened in 1973. But at the time, it had a different name. The building was called the Sears Tower until 2009 when the name changed to the Willis Tower.

Today, many different businesses have offices there. You can also go to the observation deck near the top of the building to get a great view of the city.

This building stands at the heart of Chicago, which is in the state of Illinois. Illinois is to the east of the Mississippi River. Is your community east or west of the Mississippi River?

6. Mount Rushmore

Look at the faces carved into this mountain. Do you recognize any of them? These faces also appear on coins and dollar bills.

Mount Rushmore shows the faces of four famous U.S. presidents. The faces are 60 feet high. It took 14 years to carve them. Many people visit this landmark to take pictures with these faces every year.

Mount Rushmore is in the state of South Dakota. South Dakota is west of the Mississippi River. It is east of the Rocky Mountains. Do you live east or west of the Rocky Mountains?

The faces of four U.S. presidents are carved in Mount Rushmore in South Dakota. Can you name any of these presidents?

7. The Grand Canyon

Picture yourself at the Grand Canyon. How many different colors do you notice in the rocks? How far down is the river?

How do you think the Grand Canyon got its name? A **canyon** is a deep, narrow valley with steep sides. The word *grand* means "large." The Grand Canyon is certainly large! After all, it is 277 miles long and 1 mile deep.

Many people visit the Grand Canyon just to see it. Some of them hike or ride mules to get to the bottom. A river runs along the bottom of the canyon.

The Grand Canyon is in the state of Arizona. The Colorado River is in Arizona and goes through the Grand Canyon. How far do you live from the Grand Canyon?

The Grand Canyon is 277 miles long and 1 mile deep. This famous place is found in the state of Arizona.

8. The Golden Gate Bridge

You may recognize the Golden Gate Bridge from books or television. Where can you find this famous landmark?

The Golden Gate Bridge crosses the entrance to San Francisco Bay. The bridge opened in 1937. At the time, it had the tallest towers of any bridge in the world.

The city of San Francisco is at the south end of the bridge. San Francisco is in the state of California. People cross the bridge to get to other parts of the state. If you look to the west of the bridge, you can see the Pacific Ocean. This ocean touches the West Coast of the United States. Do you live near the Pacific Ocean?

The Golden Gate Bridge is a landmark in San Francisco. San Francisco is a city in California.

Hands-On Activity Notes

Activity Online

Each of the lettered locations on this U.S. map corresponds to one of the six famous places you read about. Match the letter with the famous place.

A. califopnia	D. indiana
B. Arizona	E. ibk
C. South bakota	F. Florida

To complete the scale puzzles, do the following:

- Put a dot on the map where your community is located. Label it with the name of your community.
- Label these three places on the map: the Everglades, the Willis Tower, and Mount Rushmore.
- Use a ruler and the map scale to estimate the distance between your community and each of the three locations.
- Record your answers in the table below.

Record your scale puzzle answers here.

Location	**Distance from Your Community**
The Willis Tower	____________________ miles
Mount Rushmore	____________________ miles
The Everglades	____________________ miles

Summary

If you counted them on a map, you would find that the United States has 50 states. Maps help us find states and the places within them. You could even find your state and community with a map. When you use a map to describe where a state is found, you read the cardinal directions shown on the compass rose.

Each state has many communities and landmarks for which it is known. The Statue of Liberty, the Everglades, the Willis Tower, Mount Rushmore, the Grand Canyon, and the Golden Gate Bridge are the landmarks you learned about in this lesson. Of all these places, which one would you like to visit? Why?

Show What You Know

Think about your community. What landmark would you like your community to be known for? Draw and label it here.

Lesson 3

Geography and the Way We Live

How does geography affect our community?

Introduction

What do you think of when you hear the word *geography*? If you thought of maps and globes, you're right. People use geography skills to help them find places on a map. But geography is not just about where places are. It is also about what different places are like.

Look at this image of Boulder, Colorado. You can see how the land is shaped. Homes and buildings are located down in the valley. Tall mountains surround the valley. They are covered with trees and even snow. These things are all part of the area's geography.

In this lesson, you will read about the geography of four places in the United States. You'll learn what makes these places different from one another and how those differences affect the way people live in their community.

Vocabulary

adapt
climate
conservation
natural hazard
natural resource
physical feature
physical geography
pollution
region

This photograph of Boulder, Colorado, was taken from above. What do you notice about the shape of the land?

Preview Activity

Activity Online

Draw a picture to show what the geography of your community is like. Are there hills and mountains nearby? A river, lake, or ocean? What is the weather like? What kinds of trees or plants grow where you live?

Vocabulary Activity

Activity Online

Complete each sentence with the correct term.

Vocabulary Word Bank

climate
natural hazard
natural resources
physical feature

Land and water to grow food are examples of ______________.

A mountain or a river is an example of a ______________.

A volcano is an example of a ______________.

If a place has a lot of rain, that is part of its ______________.

Vocabulary Word Bank

adapt
conservation
physical geography
pollution
region

Buying a hat to protect you from the sun is a way to ______________.

Littering is an example of ______________.

The Northwest is an example of a ______________.

Physical features are a part of ______________.

When we are careful to recycle, we are practicing ______________.

Hands-On Activity

Create a brochure about the geography of your community. Play a matching game to find out how people in different communities adapt to geography.

Directions: Exploring Geography and Our Community

1. **Read Section 1.** Learn all about geography. Then use the interactive slideshow to discuss what you learned about physical features.
2. **Answer the questions about your community.** List the name, draw the state, and talk about the different features.
3. **Complete the brochure planning table with a partner.** Have a drawing and a sentence for each page of your brochure.
4. **Create your brochure.** Use your planning table to complete your brochure.

Directions: Exploring Other Communities

1. **Read Sections 2–6.** Learn about how and why people adapt to different kinds of physical geography. Explore different communities and learn about their geography.
2. **With a partner, examine the item on your Adaptations Card.** Read the back to learn more about the item.
3. **Look at the four communities around the classroom.** Recall the differences between them that you read about.
4. **Decide which community your item is an adaptation for.** Stand near the community's Activity Card.
5. **Prepare to share your reasoning with the class.**

1. What Is Geography?

If you went for a bus ride near your community, what would you see? Would you see tall mountains or flat plains? Would you see a lake or a river? These landforms and bodies of water are all examples of **physical features** of Earth's surface. Physical features are made by nature, not by people. They are part of the **physical geography** of the area where you live.

The geography of a place includes other things, too. For example, **climate** is a part of physical geography. Climate means what the weather in a place is like, measured over time.

Different places often have different climates. Some places get lots of rain, while others hardly ever see a cloud. Some places are icy cold in winter and boiling hot in summer. Others have mild weather almost all year-round.

Physical Features

This illustration shows different landforms and bodies of water found on Earth. These are examples of physical features.

People use many things from nature in their daily lives. These things are examples of **natural resources**. People use wood from trees to build houses, and they use land and water to grow food. These resources are also part of physical geography. What are some of the natural resources near your community?

The state of Hawaii is made of many islands. These islands are created by volcanoes.

Natural hazards play an important role in shaping Earth's geography. For example, earthquakes can knock down trees and change the shape of the land. Volcanoes can create islands. Some places have climates that cause more natural hazards like hurricanes and tornadoes. Natural hazards can change Earth's surface quickly. They are also extremely dangerous.

Hands-On Activity Notes

Activity Online

What is the name of your community?

Draw the state that your community is in.

What are the physical features of your community? Are there hills, valleys, or lakes nearby?

What are some natural resources in our community? Are there trees or water nearby?

What is our community's climate like? Is it hot and dry? Rainy?

Brochure Planning Table

Work with your partner to complete this planning table. Write your ideas for a drawing, and then write a sentence for each topic in your brochure.

	First Page	Second Page
Topic	Name and location of your community	Physical features
Drawing		
Sentence		

	Third Page	Fourth Page
Topic	Natural resources	Climate
Drawing		
Sentence		

Work with your partner to transfer information from your brochure planning table to your brochure. Remember, each page has its own topic.

People in Anchorage dress warmly because of the cold.

2. Adapting to Geography

Different kinds of physical geography have their own challenges. Water can be hard to find in areas with dry climates. Mountains can make it hard for people to travel.

People must **adapt** to the physical geography around them. Adaptation happens over time as people learn more about their surroundings.

In Anchorage, Alaska, it usually snows over 70 inches each year. People there wear warm clothes and shovel the sidewalks so that they can go outside safely. They also have cars that they can drive in the snow.

When people settle in an area, they affect their surroundings. Some of these effects are bad. Other effects are good.

Sometimes, people pollute the area around them. **Pollution** is a bad effect. Trash can enter rivers and wash up onto shores.

Overusing natural resources is another bad effect. People use natural resources, such as trees, to build homes. But if they use too many trees, they can clear large sections of forests where many plants and animals live.

People can protect the environment by using natural resources wisely. **Conservation** is a good effect. If people used fewer trees to build homes, then less land would be cleared. This would protect the plants and animals that live in that area.

This photograph of the Mississippi River shows waste that has entered the water.

3. The Geography of Roseburg, Oregon

This is an overhead view of Roseburg, Oregon. How do you think this picture was taken?

Geography has a lot to do with how we live. To see why this is so, let's look at four cities. We will start with Roseburg, Oregon.

Oregon is in the Northwest **region** of the United States. A region is an area with certain features in common. The Northwest has lots of mountains, trees, and rivers.

People in Roseburg know all about these physical features. Roseburg is in a valley of the Cascade Mountains. Tall trees cover the mountains, and a big river runs through the city. Many people go fishing in the river.

The climate in Roseburg is gentle and mild, and it rarely gets very cold or very hot. Winters are cool and rainy, while summers are warm and dry.

Roseburg's climate helps plants and trees grow. Forests are the most important natural resource in Roseburg. People work in lumber mills, cutting down trees and sending the lumber to other places. (Lumber is wood that has been cut from trees.)

Lumber mills have been in Roseburg for many years. Some people make sure that more trees are planted to replace those that are cut down. Why do you think they do this?

Logs are stacked at a lumber mill before they are shipped.

This is a view of Las Cruces, New Mexico.

4. The Geography of Las Cruces, New Mexico

The city of Las Cruces (lahs-CROO-says) is in New Mexico. This state is in the Southwest region of the United States. This is a region of sandy deserts and rugged mountains.

The geography of Las Cruces has three important physical features. First, Las Cruces is in the middle of a desert. Second, there are mountains nearby. Third, the city was built next to a river. The river is called the Rio Grande, which means "great river" in Spanish.

Las Cruces has a desert climate, so the weather is usually hot and dry. There is very little rain. In the summer, it is very hot. Temperatures can climb over 100 degrees. To stay cool, some homes in the city are built from a clay brick called adobe. Adobe keeps homes cool in the summer and warm in the winter.

Can you guess what the most important natural resource in Las Cruces is? It's water. Deserts have very little water. But people, animals, and plants all need water to live. The people in Las Cruces use their water wisely and are careful not to waste it. Where does the water come from?

The desert around Las Cruces is very dry.

The ocean is an important physical feature in Gloucester.

5. The Geography of Gloucester, Massachussetts

The city of Gloucester (GLAWS-ter) is in Massachusetts. This state is in the Northeast region of the United States. The Atlantic Ocean is to the east of this region.

The ocean is the most important physical feature near Gloucester. In fact, the city has ocean water on three sides.

People in Gloucester need lots of different clothes. The weather there changes from season to season. Summers are warm and sunny. Winters are cold and snowy. Spring and fall are cool and rainy.

The weather around Gloucester even changes from day to day. People in this part of the country say, "If you don't like the weather, wait five minutes and it will change."

Fish and other seafood are the most important natural resources in Gloucester. Since the city is close to the water, many people fish for a living. They spend many days at sea on fishing boats and then sell the fish they have caught. Other people dig for clams or trap lobsters. How have the people in Gloucester adapted to living in this area?

The weather in Gloucester can change at any moment.

Galveston is an island city. It sits off the east coast of Texas.

6. The Geography of Galveston, Texas

The city of Galveston is in the state of Texas. Texas is located in the Southwest region of the United States.

Galveston sits on an island off the coast of the Texas mainland. It is surrounded by the Gulf of Mexico. The Gulf is the most important physical feature of Galveston. Fish and crab are two key natural resources that are found in the Gulf.

Since Galveston is very close to a body of water and located closer to the equator, it gets humid there. Humidity makes the air feel wet and heavy. Texas also gets very hot in the summers. Most people have air conditioning to help cool down. However, the winters in Galveston are mild.

Since Galveston is on the coast, it is in danger of being hit by hurricanes. Hurricanes are storms that start in the ocean and often get bigger as they move toward land. Many homes in Galveston are built on stilts, or poles, to protect them from floods and winds.

But some hurricanes can do a lot of harm. In 2008, Galveston was struck by Hurricane Ike. The city became blanketed in water. The hurricane tore trees down and washed away much of Galveston's coastline. Many buildings and cars were damaged, too.

Galveston has worked hard to recover from Hurricane Ike. Natural hazards can create long-lasting damage in a short amount of time.

Natural hazards such as hurricanes can change a place's physical geography. Hurricane Ike greatly affected the city of Galveston.

Hands-On Activity Notes

Activity Online

Complete the Venn diagram to compare one of the communities you learned about with your own.

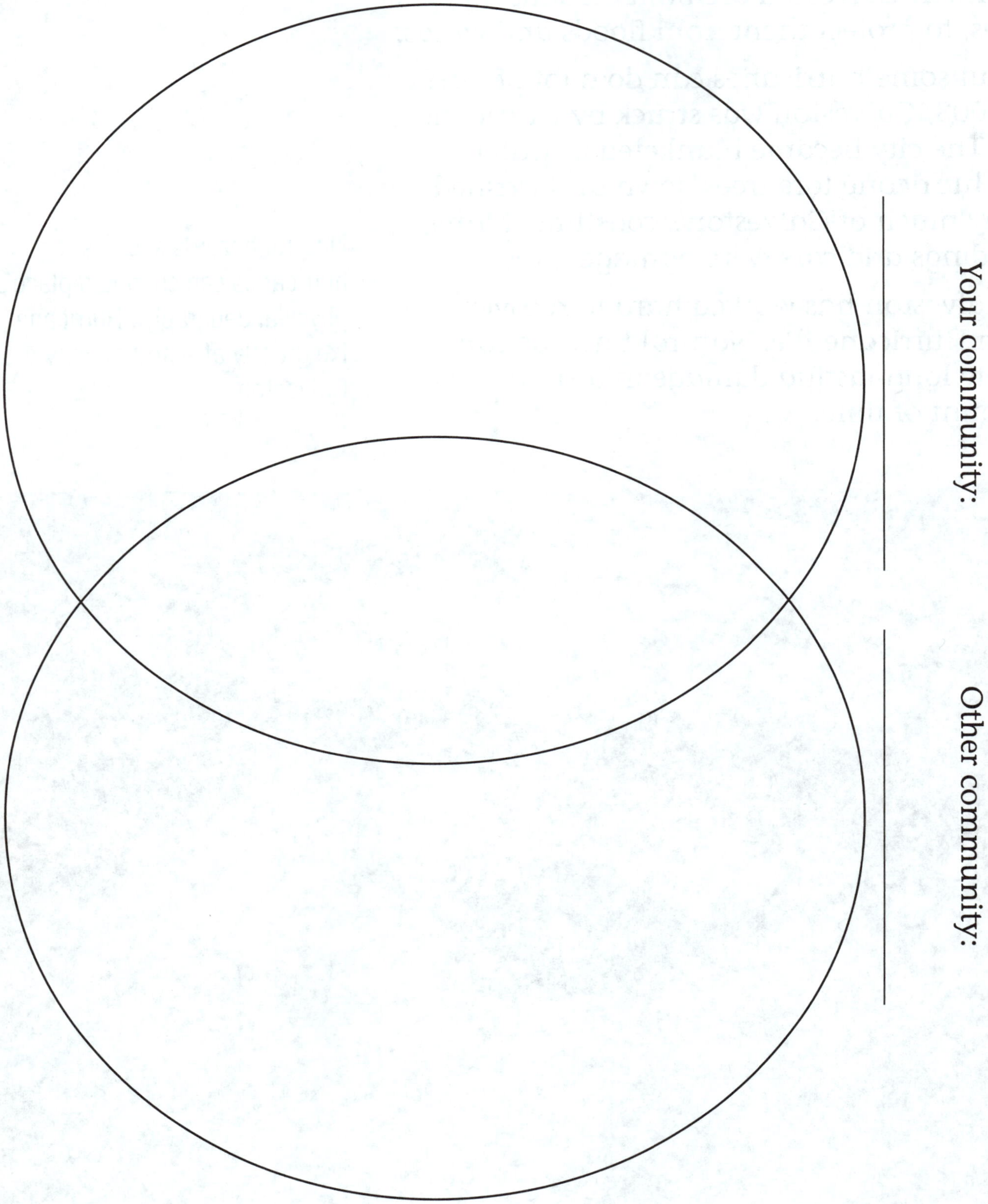

Summary

In this lesson, you learned about different physical features on Earth's surface. People in a community adapt to their environment. You also learned about four cities with different physical features, climate, and resources. All these things are part of their geography. You learned about natural hazards and how they shape Earth. Natural hazards are very dangerous.

What is the geography like where you live? Do you think any of it has been shaped by hazards? Can you think of any natural resources in your area?

Show What You Know

Think about your community's physical features, climate, and natural resources. Then draw two ways that you and your family have adapted to your community's geography.

Describe how your community adapts to these parts of geography: physical features, climate, and natural resources.

Lesson 4

Native Americans and Their Environments

How did Native Americans adapt to the environment long ago?

Introduction

What do you think life in North America was like 600 years ago? At the time, many Native American groups lived across the continent. They did not have grocery stores, cars, or electricity. They relied on their environment to get what they needed.

There are many types of environments in North America. Each Native American group developed a way of life based on where they lived. Some made canoes and fished, while others followed herds of bison for food and shelter. They ate food and built houses based on what they could find around them. However, their way of life changed when Europeans arrived in North America.

In this lesson, you will learn about how different Native American groups used their environment long ago. You will find out how European colonists changed the way Native Americans lived.

Vocabulary

environment

trade

tribe

How did Native Americans from long ago use their environment to make this structure?

Preview Activity

Activity Online

Draw a symbol or simple sketch of each environment in the correct box.

Vocabulary Activity

Activity Online

Read the description about Native American life in North America. Fill in the blanks with words from the word bank.

Vocabulary Word Bank

environment **trade** **tribes**

An elder of the Koskimo Native American community from the Pacific Northwest Coast rubs a a wooden stick between his hands to make a fire to cook food.

What do you think life in North America was like 600 years ago? At the time, many Native American groups, or ____________________ , lived across the continent. They were each surrounded by different types of air, water, soil, and living things, or a different ____________________ . No matter where Native American groups lived, they adapted to the environment. Each tribe made goods from their environment. They could then ____________________ the goods they made with other tribes to get things they normally could not make.

Hands-On Activity

Activity Online

Learn how different Native American groups adapted to their environments by finding hidden objects and organisms in six different locations.

Directions: Observing Native American Environments

1. **With a partner, look through the first environment to find the four hidden objects or organisms.** Look closely! Listen to the audio for each item you find.
2. **Read Section 1.** Take notes and highlight anything that stands out to you.
3. **As a class, discuss how that Native American group adapted to their environment.** Use evidence from the text or audio clips to support your claim.
4. **Complete the Activity Notes for the first environment.**
5. **Repeat Steps 1–4 to explore the remaining five environments.**

This picture shows a replica of a longhouse that the Chinook people lived in long ago. How did the Chinooks use the environment around them to build shelters?

1. Chinooks

The Chinook people lived along the Pacific Coast in what is now Washington and Oregon. There were many rivers, trees, and bushes in their **environment**.

The Chinook people adapted to their environment. Because they lived near oceans and rivers, they built canoes to fish. Salmon were plentiful in the area and made up a large part of their diet. They also gathered nuts and berries from the plants around them.

Many Chinook families lived together in longhouses. Longhouses are large houses made from cedar planks. More than 50 people lived in each longhouse. They slept on mats made from reeds.

The Chinook people **traded** with other Native American groups. They exchanged salmon and decorative shells for other goods.

Today, many Chinook people still live in Washington and Oregon. They formed a government and are seeking to be recognized as a **tribe**.

The Chinook people lived by the Pacific Ocean.

Where the Chinooks Lived

These ovens were found in New Mexico. The Utes living there used the earth and clay in the area to build them.

2. Utes

Utah is named after the Ute people. The Utes lived in the Great Basin area, which includes Colorado and Utah. The environment was dry but had many mountains, valleys, and lakes.

The Utes adapted to their environment by hunting and gathering food in the area. Animals such as bison, elk, and rabbit lived nearby. The Utes used tools such as arrows, spears, and nets to hunt them. They also gathered nuts, seeds, and berries for food.

The Utes lived in different types of houses, depending on what they could find in their environment. Some lived in tepees made from hide. Others who lived near willow trees made dome-shaped homes from them.

The Utes made different goods. They made ovens from mud and clay to cook food. They used animal hide to make leather clothes and bags. They coiled willow leaves for baskets, which they used to store food and water.

Today, there are three tribes within the Ute nation. The Ute language is still spoken on reservations, and some tribes have annual dances to keep traditions alive. The Ute people are involved in tourism, timber, and oil industries.

The Ute people lived in the Great Basin.

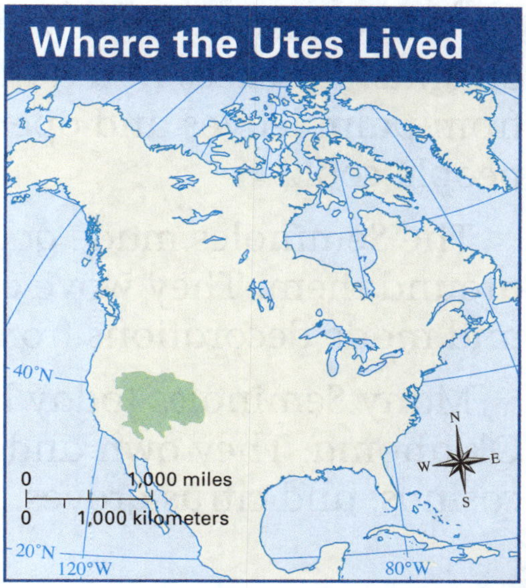

To stay cool, the Seminoles lived in open-air homes called *chickees.*

3. Seminoles

The Seminoles people lived in the swamplands of Florida. Many of them came from the Creek tribe, but people from other nearby groups joined them over time. In the 1800s, they were joined by African Americans who had escaped slavery. Together, these groups defended their land against American colonizers.

The Seminoles lived in a hot and wet environment. They adapted to it by growing crops, including corn, beans, and squash. They also fished using canoes made from hollowed-out cypress trees.

To adapt to the swamplands, the Seminoles lived in chickees. These were houses raised on stilts. Chickees had a thatched roof made from palm leaves and open sides to help keep people cool.

The Seminoles made goods from the things around them. They wove clothes and baskets and made decorations from beads.

Many Seminoles today live in Florida and Oklahoma. They own and operate hotels, casinos, and citrus groves.

The Seminole people lived in the swamplands of Florida.

Where the Seminoles Lived

Yucca plants grew in the desert. The Yaquis used yucca fibers to make sandals.

4. Yaquis

The Yaqui people lived in a hot and dry environment in what is now Mexico. Some lived near a river, but others lived in the desert and mountains.

The Yaquis adapted to these environments. Those who lived by a river were farmers. They grew crops on land that the river flooded each year. Those who lived in the desert and mountains were hunters and gatherers. They hunted animals such as deer and rabbits.

To keep cool, the Yaquis lived in houses with open sides covered with cane mats. The mats were held up by poles. Some built houses with walls made from cane and mud.

The Yaquis made clothing that kept them cool. They made sandals from yucca fibers. They also made beaded necklaces and wove blankets.

Many Yaqui tribe members live in Mexico and Arizona today. Older tribe members pass on traditions to younger generations. They teach younger members the Yaqui language and ritual dances.

The Yaqui people live in parts of Mexico and Arizona.

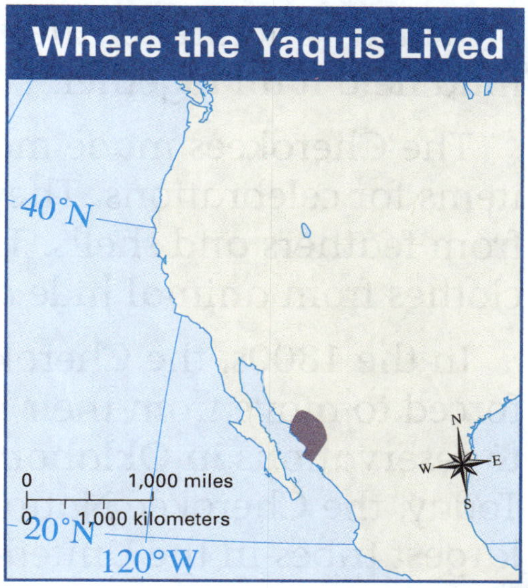

The Cherokees sometimes used blowguns to hunt for birds and small animals in the area. This person demonstrates how to use a traditional blowgun.

5. Cherokees

The Cherokee people lived in what is now Tennessee and North Carolina. They lived in the woodlands with many rivers, mountains, and valleys.

The Cherokees grew crops for food. They grew herbs, sunflowers, and squash. They would hunt, as well, and use all the parts of the animal. Bears, elk, and deer were some of the animals they hunted. Hunters wore deerskin as a disguise to sneak up on their prey.

Some Cherokee groups lived in log cabins that had a hole in the roof for smoke to escape. Others lived in wattle and daub houses made from sticks and mud. The sticks provided structure for the houses, while the mud held it all together.

The Cherokees made many decorative items for celebrations. They made accessories from feathers and shells. They also made clothes from animal hide and hair.

In the 1800s, the Cherokee people were forced to move from their homes and relocate to reservations in Oklahoma and Arkansas. Today, the Cherokee Nation is one of the largest tribes in the United States.

The Cherokee people adapted to the environment of the Appalachian Mountains.

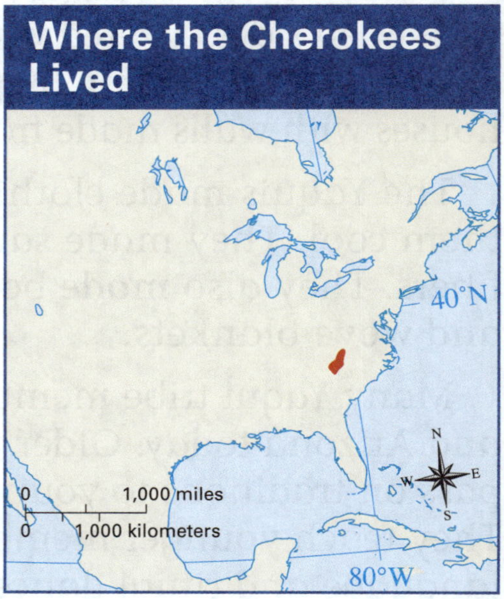

Some groups of Sioux made clothing from bison hide. This person wears a replica of a bison coat.

6. Sioux

The Sioux is an alliance between several Native American groups, including the Dakota and Lakota. These groups lived in and around what is now Wisconsin and Minnesota, but some traveled west. Others settled near Lake Superior.

The Sioux relied on their environment for food. Some groups gathered wild rice, hunted, and used canoes to fish. Others farmed and grew corn. These groups would trade food and resources with each other.

Bison were an important part of Sioux life. Some Sioux groups followed bison so they would have a supply of food. They lived in tepees, or tents made from bison. They also made robes and created calendars from bison hide.

The Sioux also created many other goods. They made beads and other decorative items from porcupine quills.

Today, there are Sioux reservations in Minnesota, North Dakota, South Dakota, Montana, and Nebraska. Many Sioux people live off their reservations.

The Sioux people primarily live in the Great Plains.

Where the Sioux Lived

After Europeans brought horses to North America, some Native American groups adapted to use horses. This early 1900s photo shows Sioux people riding horses.

7. Native Americans and European Colonists

Europeans came to North America in the late 1400s. They formed communities and settlements on the East Coast. Over time, they moved west. Their arrival changed how Native Americans lived.

When Europeans arrived, they brought with them goods and animals that were new to Native Americans. For example, they brought horses and sheep to North America. Some tribes would get horses of their own to make hunting easier.

However, Europeans also brought diseases. Many Native Americans got sick and died from these diseases. The Native American population decreased significantly. Many tribes were destroyed.

As European colonists and Native American groups came into contact, both positive and negative relationships were formed. They traded fur and other goods with each other. Some Native Americans helped the Europeans get used to their new environment by teaching them how to fish and plant corn. Some alliances were formed. But many conflicts also arose.

As Europeans built colonies and settlements along the East Coast, Native American groups were forced off their home land. They had to find new places to live. Many of them moved west and had to adapt to a new environment.

Over time, European colonists also moved west. They encountered more tribes, began trading with them, and also displaced them. The way of life that Native Americans had known for centuries began to disappear. Native Americans struggled to hold on to their traditions.

Native American groups continue to keep their traditions alive. Here, Sioux children gather to celebrate their heritage.

Hands-On Activity Notes

Activity Online

Explore each environment online. Then record at least two ways each Native American group adapted to their environment. Provide examples.

Chinooks: Pacific Coast (Section 1)

Utes: The Great Basin (Section 2)

Seminoles: Swamplands of Florida (Section 3)

Yaquis: Sonoran Desert (Section 4)

Cherokees: Appalachian Mountains (Section 5)

Sioux: Great Plains (Section 6)

Summary

Many Native American groups lived across North America 600 years ago. Each group developed a way of life based on their environment. They adapted to their environment to get food, build shelters, and make clothes.

Groups that lived near oceans and rivers fished. Those who lived in hot areas built shelters that helped them stay cool. Some groups who lived in the plains followed bison herds.

However, their way of life changed when Europeans arrived in North America. Europeans introduced horses to Native Americans, but they also brought diseases that killed large numbers of them. Native Americans had to adapt to life with European colonists.

Show What You Know

Pick one artifact you would like to analyze and circle it. Then answer the questions about the artifact on the next page.

Culture: Which Native American tribe does the artifact belong to?

Claim: Which environment was the artifact created for?

Evidence: What connects this artifact to its environment?

Reasoning: How does the evidence prove your claim?

Unit 2

History

Analyze primary sources to explore immigration throughout U.S. history. Study the characteristics of culture and play a game themed on your community. Honor a citizen-leader who improved their community. Travel to other countries to learn about their cultures. Conduct an inquiry to investigate how history and culture influence your community.

Unit Inquiry Project

1 Gathering Visual Evidence

What do you see in this image?	
What do you think is happening in this image? Give evidence.	
Why might Americans celebrate a holiday that comes from the country of Ireland?	

2 Developing the Compelling Question

Unit Storyline

This is a St. Patrick's Day celebration outside of Boston, Massachusetts. St. Patrick's Day is an Irish holiday. Many Irish people moved to large cities like Boston in the 1800s. Over the years, many other ethnic groups have settled in the United States as well. How does the history of settlement impact the customs where people choose to live? How is your community's culture related to its history?

Unit Compelling Question

How do history and culture shape your community?

List three questions you have about the Unit Storyline and Compelling Question.

1.

2.

3.

3 Collecting Evidence

After you complete each lesson, return to this table and answer the questions. You will be gathering key information that will help you complete the Unit Inquiry Project.

Lesson	Supporting Questions	What I Learned
5 Settling in the United States	Why do people move from one country to another? What indigenous groups lived in your area? What groups have come from elsewhere around the world?	
6 Diversity in the United States	Why is diversity important in the United States? What cultural traditions are celebrated in your community?	
7 Making Communities Better	What are some ways that people have helped their communities in the past? Who are people that have made your community a better place?	
8 Cultures Around the World	What can visiting another country tell you about its history and culture? Compare your community's history and culture to another community around the world.	

4 Building Additional Content Knowledge

Gather and evaluate additional sources to answer the Unit Compelling Question: *How do history and culture shape your community?*

You may conduct outside research or use these readings from *Social Studies Alive! Our Community and Beyond* Social Studies Stories:

- Many People, Many Ways of Life
- Europeans Learn About North America
- The Story of Mexico City
- Making Mail Faster
- Benjamin Franklin, Public Servant

Source Title(s)	
Additional Evidence	

5 Constructing an Argument

Write a sentence answering the Unit Compelling Question: *How do history and culture shape your community?* This is called a claim.

Then provide at least two pieces of evidence to support your claim. Your evidence can come from the activities you did in class, the readings you completed in your Student Journal or Social Studies Stories, or additional research that you conducted.

Claim:

Evidence:

6 Taking Informed Action

Decide how you want to share what you learned. You could make a poster, a digital presentation, or a video. You might share your presentation with your classmates or with adults in the community.

Lesson 5

Settling in the United States

How do people become part of our country?

Introduction

People from many different places live in the United States. But how did we all get here? Native Americans have lived here for thousands of years. But many groups of people have come much more recently to the United States.

Europeans began to come here about 500 years ago. They brought captive African people over in the 1600s. Since then, people have come from many different countries. Today, people from all over the world come to the United States.

In this lesson, you will read about the history of people in this country. You will find out about people who came to the Americas before 1800. You will find out why people kept coming after 1800. You will learn about the challenges they faced when they arrived. Finally, you will explore how people who come here become part of our country.

Vocabulary

citizen

discriminate

immigrant

Immigrants arrive at Ellis Island, New York, in the early 1900s. Why did these people come to the United States?

The Tlingit people built canoes to travel and fish along the Pacific Coast. People who settled in the Great Plains used buffalo skin to build shelters.

1. America Before 1800

The first group of people to live in North America came thousands of years ago. They are the ancestors of Native Americans. Evidence suggests that the first Americans came at least 11,500 years ago.

Scientists think that the first Americans traveled from Asia to North America to look for food. They may have followed herds of animals that wandered into the Americas. When the first Americans arrived, they used the environment around them to find food and make shelters.

For thousands of years, the first Americans built settlements across the Americas. Many different communities formed with their own ways of life. The Tlinglit people lived and fished along the Pacific Coast. People who settled in the Great Plains hunted buffalo.

In 1492, the Taíno people living in the Caribbean saw three ships landing on the shore. The ships belonged to an explorer named Christopher Columbus. Columbus sailed from Spain to look for spices and gold. He and his men took over the land. They killed and enslaved many indigenous people to do this.

Soon, Spain started a colony in the Caribbean. They enslaved native people and forced them to plant sugarcane, tobacco, and rice. Later, they brought captive African people to grow crops. Many other European countries followed Spain and colonized other parts of the Americas.

In 1619, African people were enslaved and brought to Virginia. They were brought against their will by English settlers and forced to work for them. African people in the Americas had a difficult life. It would be hundreds of years before slavery would end here.

These groups of people came to the Americas before the United States became a country in 1776. After 1800, many more people came here. Why did people keep coming?

What groups came to the Americas before 1800?

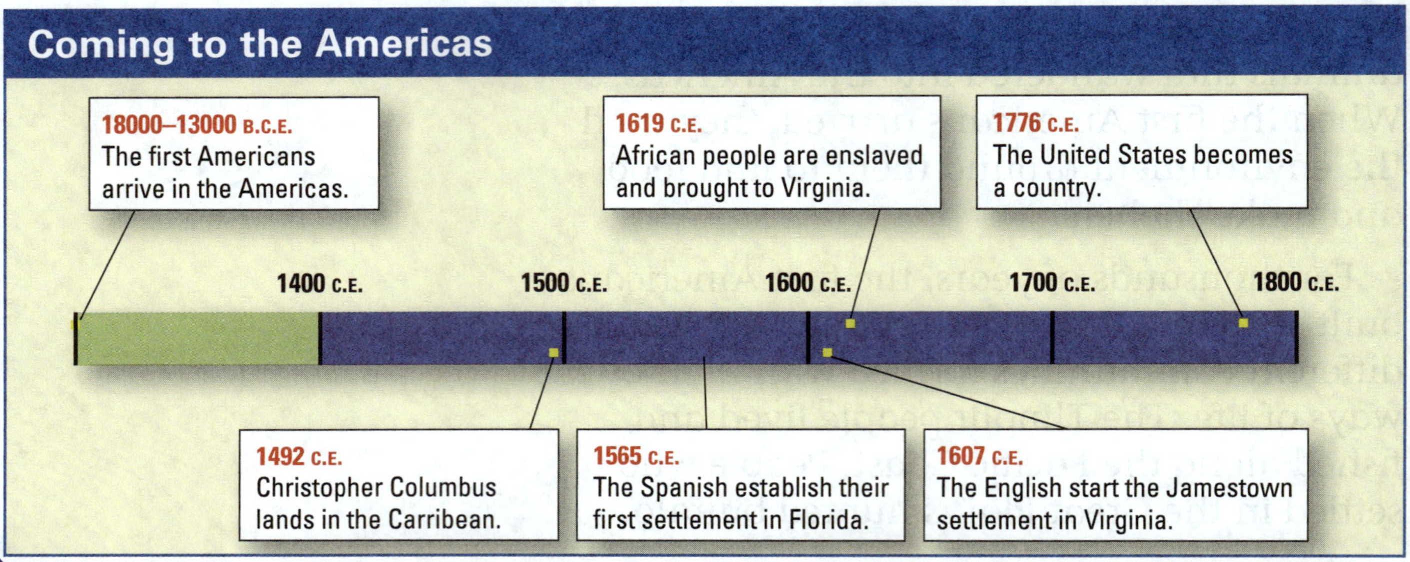

Preview Activity

Activity Online

Think of a time you moved to a new place. Draw how you felt.

Listen to the three audio clips. You will hear immigrants telling a small part of their stories.

Record questions that you have about immigration.

1. ______________________________

____

____

2. ______________________________

____

____

3. ______________________________

____

____

Vocabulary Activity

Activity Online

Fill out the table for each of the terms.

Term	Describe It	Use It in a Sentence
citizen		
discriminate		
immigrant		

Hands-On Activity

Activity Online

Investigate immigration in the United States by carefully analyzing visual and written primary sources from various time periods.

Directions: Analyzing Primary Sources

1. **With a partner, read Section 2.** Take turns reading the section to learn why people decide to move to the United States.
2. **In your Activity Notes, write down the main idea of this section.** Summarize the main point of the section in one sentence.
3. **Walk around the room to look at the primary sources. Record the letters of the primary sources that match this section.** On each Activity Card, look for visual clues in the image. Then read the caption. If the topic matches this section, record its letter. If not, keep looking. There are four sources for each section.
4. **How would you describe the primary sources for this section? Decide on one adjective.**
5. **Repeat these steps for Sections 3–6.**

2. Why Immigrants Come to the United States

This engraving shows Irish immigrants on a ship bound for the United States. Many people left Ireland because of a disease that killed potato plants.

When people move to another country to live, they are called **immigrants**. Immigrants come to the United States for many reasons. Sometimes, they need to get away from problems. There might be wars or unfair laws where they live. Sometimes, there are too many people in a place without enough jobs or food for everyone.

Once, a disease started to kill all the potato plants in Ireland. Potatoes were an important food in that country. When the plants died, people began to starve. Many families left their homes and moved to the United States.

After the Irish, many immigrants from other countries fled to the United States. Millions of Italians came to the United States to escape poverty. Jewish immigrants from Eastern Europe came to evade unfair treatment. And Mexicans came to avoid a bloody civil war.

But people do not move here just to escape problems. Often, they simply want a chance for a better life. That is one reason our country grew so quickly in the 1800s.

Many people came from Europe to get good jobs or to start farms. When gold was discovered in California, people rushed to the gold fields from all over the world. Only a few of them got rich, but many stayed anyway. Can you think of some reasons why people might want to come to the United States today?

Thousands of people rushed to the gold fields in California hoping to make a fortune.

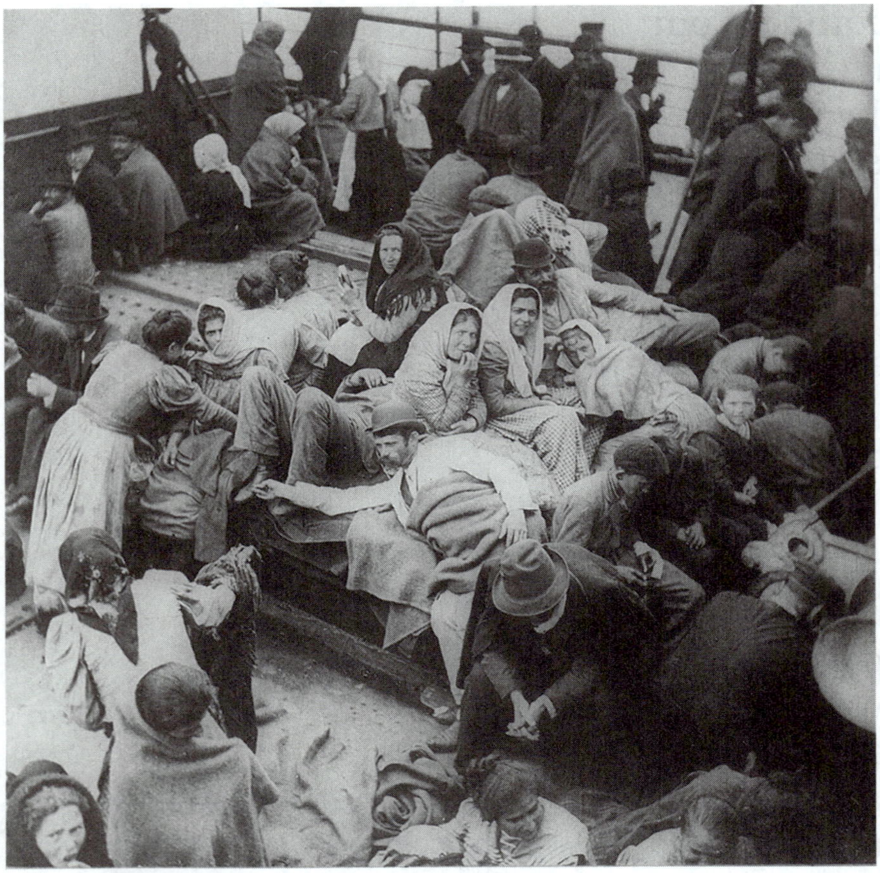

Immigrants traveled to America by ship. Filthy toilets sometimes made the ship smell so bad that passengers crowded onto the main deck for fresh air.

3. How Immigrants Come to the United States

Getting to the United States is often very hard for immigrants. In the past, people came from Asia and Europe on crowded ships. These people included the Irish, the Jews, and the Chinese.

Often, the conditions on the ships were awful. The ships were unsanitary and overcrowded with passengers. A ship might take weeks to cross the ocean. But not all immigrants traveled to the United States by sea. People from Mexico and other places sometimes walked hundreds of miles.

Things were not easy after the trip was over, either. Government officials tested new immigrants to see if they were healthy. If they were sick, they could be sent home.

Immigrants also had to answer a lot of questions. They had to say where they were going to stay and show how they were going to make a living. They did not always have good answers and were turned away. But millions were allowed to stay.

Today, getting to the United States is a lot easier because of airplanes. But it is even harder to stay.

Before coming to the United States, immigrants must get permission to stay here. They have to hire lawyers and fill out lots of papers. The process is expensive and can take years. Sometimes, entire families save money so just one person can immigrate. Often, they hope that the rest of the family can come later.

Immigrants had to show they were healthy. These immigrants are having their eyes checked for disease.

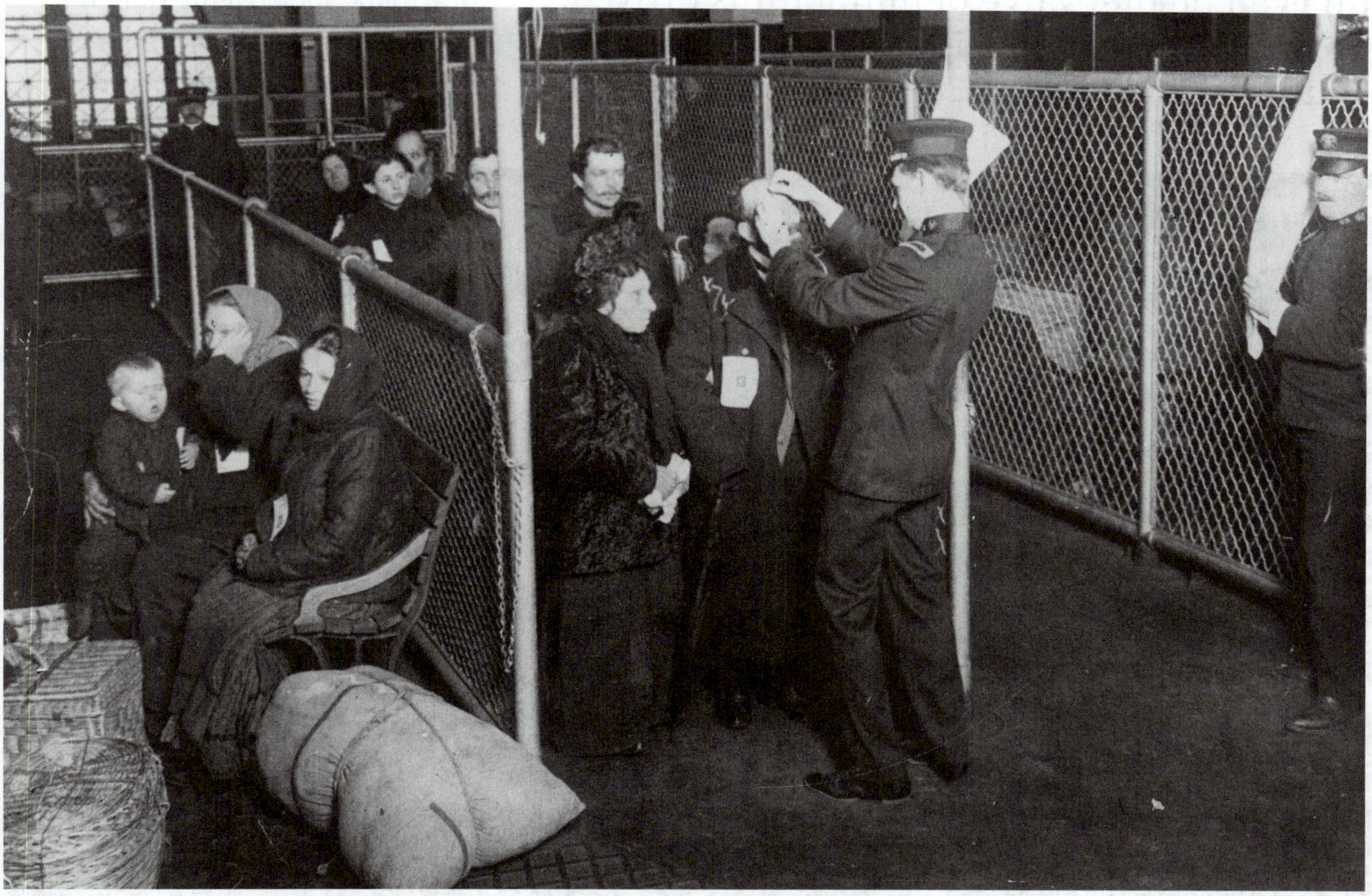

4. Settling in the United States

People from all over the world have immigrated to the United States. But they did not all come at the same time, and they did not all settle in the same place.

About 170 years ago, many immigrants came to the United States from Ireland and Germany. They crossed the Atlantic Ocean and arrived on the East Coast of the United States.

There were a lot of jobs available in northeastern cities, and the Irish tended to settle in cities such as New York City, Boston, and Philadelphia. Germans, who usually had more money than the Irish, often moved west and became farmers.

After the Irish and Germans first came, an even greater wave of immigrants arrived. This time, most of the immigrants came from Southern and Eastern Europe.

Immigrants often settled in northeastern cities where they found jobs. Many Italian immigrants lived in Little Italies such as this one in New York City.

Immigrants from the same country often settled in the same neighborhoods. Italians in New York City settled in their own neighborhoods called Little Italies. Jewish immigrants flocked to the Lower East Side of New York City, where many made clothes for a living.

Chinese immigrants crossed the Pacific Ocean and arrived on the West Coast. They came to California seeking gold. They often settled in neighborhoods like Chinatown in San Francisco.

Many Mexicans lived in California and the Southwest before that region became part of the United States. Later, more Mexicans came to those states and worked on farms or railroads.

Today, most immigrants come from Asia and Latin America. Are there immigrants in your community? Where are they from?

Many Chinese immigrants settled in California city neighborhoods, such as Chinatown in San Francisco.

Immigrants often work long hours in difficult jobs. Many of them endure unfair wages and working conditions.

5. Life for Immigrants in the United States

Many immigrants come to the United States for a better future, but starting life in a new country can be hard. Sometimes people **discriminate** against immigrants. To discriminate means to treat people unfairly because they belong to a different group.

When groups of immigrants first arrived, they needed jobs and housing. But many hospitals did not hire Jewish doctors, and housing was closed to Chinese immigrants in many areas. Many Italians were treated like criminals because a few Italians had become famous criminals. And many Mexican immigrants were paid very low wages.

Immigrants today face challenges, too. Some immigrants have to take jobs that no one else wants. These jobs can be dangerous. Often, the jobs do not pay much money. Many immigrants work long hours to earn the money they need.

Immigrants also find good things about life here. They may have more freedom than they had before. If they work hard, they may get better jobs. Then they and their children can have even better lives in the United States.

Some immigrants are famous in our country. Albert Einstein, an award-winning scientist, came here from Germany. Einstein was a Jew, and at the time, Germany was a dangerous place for Jews to live. He came to our country for protection.

Pramila Jayapal is a member of the U.S. House of Representatives. She has served since 2017. She was born in Chennai, India and is the first South Asian American woman elected to Congress.

Albert Einstein (left) and Pramila Jayapal (right) both immigrated to the United States. Many immigrants choose to come to this country in search of more opportunities.

Immigrants become American citizens in ceremonies like this one. How do immigrants become part of our country?

6. Becoming a U.S. Citizen

Suppose you are an immigrant to the United States. You have traveled all the way here for a better life. You want to live in the United States for the rest of your life. But first, you must become a U.S. citizen.

A **citizen** is a person who has the right to live in a certain place. So, a U.S. citizen is a person who has the right to live in the United States. There are two ways to become a U.S. citizen: by birth or through law.

To become a U.S. citizen at birth, you must be born in the United States or have parents who are U.S. citizens. Most immigrants do not meet these standards. They are not born in the United States, and their parents are usually not U.S. citizens. So, most immigrants must become citizens through law.

Becoming a citizen through law can take years. To qualify, you must be 18 or older. You have to live in the United States for at least five years. You need to apply and take a test on American history and the English language. Only after you pass the test will you become a U.S. citizen. An immigrant can also qualify to apply for citizenship by marrying a U.S. citizen or joining the military.

Not all immigrants become U.S. citizens. About half of the immigrants in the United States are now U.S. citizens. They call America home.

This is a certificate making an immigrant from Portugal a U.S. citizen. It took him years to get it.

United States of America, } ss.
Eastern District of New York.

97-295

Be It Remembered That at a District Court of the United States of America, held in and for the Eastern District of New York, on the sixth day of September in the year of our Lord, one thousand nine hundred and six John B. Palmeira at present of the Borough of Brooklyn City and State of New York, having appeared in said Court and applied to be admitted a **Citizen of the United States of America,** pursuant to the directions of the Act of the Congress of the United States of America, entitled "An Act to establish an uniform rule of Naturalization, etc.," passed April 14th, 1802, and Acts subsequently passed on that subject, and to the directions of the Act of Congress, entitled "An Act To regulate the immigration of aliens into the United States," approved March 3rd, 1903, and having thereupon produced to the Court such evidence, and made such declaration, renunciation and affidavits as are by the said Acts required, and the same having been duly recorded as provided by said Acts, it was Thereupon Ordered by the said Court that he be admitted, and he was accordingly admitted to be a **Citizen of the United States of America.**

Signature of Applicant
John B. Palmeira

In [illegible]ony Whereof, the seal of the said Court is hereunto affixed this 6 day of September in the year of our [illegible]d, one thousand nine hundred and six, and of our independence the one hundred and thirty-first

Clerk.

Hands-On Activity Notes

Activity Online

For each section, complete the notes. You will need to use the Activity Cards posted around the classroom.

Section 2: Why Immigrants Come to the United States

Main Idea: ______________________________

____

Primary Sources: ☐ ☐ ☐ ☐

Adjective: ______________________________

Section 3: How Immigrants Come to the United States

Main Idea: ______________________________

____

Primary Sources: ☐ ☐ ☐ ☐

Adjective: ______________________________

Section 4: Settling in the United States

Main Idea: ______________________________

____

Primary Sources: ☐ ☐ ☐ ☐

Adjective: ______________________________

Section 5: Life for Immigrants in the United States

Main Idea: ______________________________

____

Primary Sources: ☐ ☐ ☐ ☐

Adjective: ______________________________

Section 6: Becoming a U.S. Citizen

Main Idea: ______________________________

____

Primary Sources: ☐ ☐ ☐ ☐

Adjective: ______________________________

Summary

Immigrants come to the United States for many reasons. Some want to get away from problems. Others hope for a good job or more freedom. After arriving here, immigrants often settle where they can find jobs. They also settle in places where other immigrants from the same country live.

Being an immigrant can be hard. Immigrants may face discrimination. It can take a long time for them to adjust to a new home. But many people around the world believe that coming to the United States is their best chance for a better life.

Show What You Know

Think about what you have learned. Fill in the chart by describing at least three opportunities and at least three challenges of immigration.

Immigrating to the United States

Opportunities	Challenges

Lesson 6

Diversity in the United States

What different groups of people make up our culture?

Introduction

Think about what it is like to live in a big city like New York. If you walk down the street, you may see many types of restaurants. You might hear people speaking different languages and see people playing different games. These differences are a result of the many cultures that exist in a city.

A culture is a way of life that a group of people shares. The people in the group have things in common. They may be from the same country or practice the same religion. These people have a certain culture. A group may have languages, foods, music, and games that are part of its culture.

Our country is a very diverse place. *Diverse* means "made up of different groups of people or cultures." In this lesson, you will explore some of the things that different cultures bring to our nation and communities.

Vocabulary

culture

diverse

These Americans are celebrating Thanksgiving during a parade in New York City.

Preview Activity

Activity Online

For each category, find, circle, and label at least one example you see in the image. An example has been done for you.

Foods   Languages   Holidays

Traditions   Arts

Arts

Vocabulary Activity

Activity Online

Complete the definition web for each term.

Glossary Definition

In Your Own Words

Culture

Why do you think culture is important?

Glossary Definition

In Your Own Words

Diverse

Why do you think diversity is important?

Hands-On Activity

Explore cultural diversity by looking at the contributions of different cultures in the categories of foods, languages, holidays, traditions, and the arts. Play a game to brainstorm cultural contributions in your community.

Directions: Categories of Culture

1. **Watch the video and read Section 1.**
2. **Record the categories of culture and one example of each in your Activity Notes.** Use information from the video or from the text.
3. **Read Sections 2–6 and add at least one more example to 0each category.**
4. **Conduct research about culture in your local community.**

Directions: The Culture Game

1. **Get into teams of three.** Review the categories of culture you've learned.
2. **Play the Culture Game.** Follow the rules on the slides. You will brainstorm items that come from different cultures. To earn a point, your items should:
    - start with the correct letter
    - be connected to one of these categories: foods, languages, holidays, traditions, or arts
    - be unique (no other group lists it)
3. **Debrief.** Describe one unique item from your list—what culture it comes from, what it is made of, when it is eaten, how it is celebrated, and so on.

European immigrants pack a ship headed for the United States. What reasons did they have for coming to the United States?

1. Our Community Shares Different Cultures

If you go to New York City, you may notice many different groups of people. You may also notice different food, music, and languages. Why is this place so **diverse**?

People came to this country from all over the world. They came to improve their lives or to get away from problems. Many sailed from Europe to places like New York City. Others were enslaved and forced to come from Africa.

People came from other countries, too. Some sailed from Asia to the West Coast. Others traveled north from Mexico and South America.

The places that immigrants come from have different ways of life, or **cultures**. Different things make up culture. A culture shares certain foods, languages, holidays, and traditions. When immigrants arrive in the United States, they bring parts of their culture with them. Bits and pieces of these cultures find their way into American culture. This makes our country diverse.

There are many different types of food, languages, holidays, and traditions in American culture because so many different groups came to this country. The food we eat comes from different places. So do the games we play and the music we listen to. Even some holidays that Americans celebrate come from different cultures.

You may have friends from all types of cultures. People from different cultures may go to the same school as you. They may celebrate some of the same holidays as you. The way they live and the way you live help make up American culture.

In the United States, people come from different countries, but they share parts of their cultures with each other. What foods, languages, holidays, and traditions make up our culture?

Students in class with you may come from many different cultural backgrounds.

Hands-On Activity Notes

Activity Online

Follow these steps to complete the table:

1. First, watch the video. Record the five categories of culture, and give one example for each category.
2. Then, read Sections 2–6 and record at least one more example in each category.
3. Finally, conduct research about your community. Record at least one more example in each category based on your research.

Category	Examples
	1.
	2.
	3.
	1.
	2.
	3.

Category	Examples
	1.
	2.
	3.
	1.
	2.
	3.
	1.
	2.
	3.

2. Our Community Shares Different Foods

You're walking down a street in New York. Each restaurant you pass is different. One is Italian, and the next one is Chinese.

Food is an important part of any culture. When people move to a new place, they often keep making the foods they are used to eating. Many communities have people from different cultures, so they also have many kinds of foods.

Many popular foods come from Europe. Do you like gingerbread? Europeans have made it for hundreds of years. Spaghetti comes from the Italian culture, and bagels come from the Jewish culture in Europe.

Have you ever tasted borscht? It is a soup made from beets. Borscht comes from the Russian culture. How about a gyro (YEE-roh)? A gyro is a sandwich made with roasted meat and pita bread. It comes from the Greek culture.

Bagels, a very popular food in the United States, come from Jewish culture.

People often eat food that is from a culture other their own. At this Italian restaurant in New York City, many of the people eating may not have an Italian background.

Some restaurants in the United States serve a Vietnamese dish called pho, which is a soup of noodles and meat.

Asian Americans also have brought their foods to the United States. Do you like Japanese sushi? Or Chinese chow mein (chow-MAYN)? What about pho? Pho is a soup of noodles and meat. It comes from the country of Vietnam. Have you ever had tandoori chicken? This spicy dish comes from India.

Many popular foods come from Latin American cultures. These are the cultures of Mexico, Central America, and South America. For instance, you may like tacos and tamales (tuh-MAH-leez). They come from the Mexican culture.

African Americans share other foods. Hoppin' John is a stew of pork, rice, and black-eyed peas.

What are some of the foods that people eat where you live? From what cultures do these foods come?

3. Our Community Shares Different Languages

Most people in the United States speak English. But many of us also use other languages. If you visit neighborhoods across the country, you may see signs in Chinese or hear people speak Spanish.

Many Americans from Arab families live in Dearborn, Michigan. You may see Arabic signs or hear the Arabic language there. In some California neighborhoods, you may hear people speak Vietnamese. Immigrants from Vietnam settled in these places. Millions of Latinos live in Texas and throughout the country. They may speak Spanish in their homes and with friends.

You probably speak some of these languages, even if you don't know it! That's because we get many English words from other languages. *Algebra* comes from Arabic. *Guitar* and *mosquito* are from Spanish. The names of many places also come from Spanish. *Florida* comes from the Spanish word meaning "flowers."

This neighborhood has street signs in two languages, English and Chinese.

Some stores sell newspapers in many languages.

We get words from many other languages, too. For example, the word *banana* is a West African word. The word *cookie* comes from Dutch. And the word *pretzel* is a German word.

Long before Europeans came to our land, many Native American groups lived here. They had hundreds of languages. People still speak some of these languages today, such as Navajo and Cherokee. Some English words and names come from these languages, too. *Skunk* is one example, and another is *Kentucky*.

What about where you live? What are some languages that you hear in your community?

4. Our Community Shares Different Holidays

These dancers are part of a Cinco de Mayo celebration. Cinco de Mayo is a holiday that comes from Mexican culture.

Do you like holidays? Holidays are more than days when we do not have to go to school or work. They are days when we honor important people and events.

Each culture has its own special days. Many of our holidays came to us from Europe. One is Valentine's Day. Europeans have celebrated this day for hundreds of years. The Irish brought us St. Patrick's Day.

Some days are important in more than one culture. For Japanese Americans, the fifth of May is Children's Day. For Mexican Americans, the same day is Cinco de Mayo (SINK-oh day MY-oh). This holiday honors a famous battle in Mexican history.

December is a month full of holidays. Kwanzaa honors the culture of African Americans and lasts for a week. Jewish people celebrate the eight days of Hanukkah. People in many Christian cultures share the holiday of Christmas.

We celebrate the new year in different ways, too. For many of us, New Year's Day is the first day of January. For many Chinese people, the new year starts on a different date each year. The Chinese New Year celebration goes on for 15 days.

What holidays do people celebrate where you live? Which ones do you share with your family and friends?

Many people like to light candles for Kwanzaa, a holiday that honors African American culture.

5. Our Community Shares Different Traditions

You can see people take part in activities that happen every year. These activities are traditions. What traditions do Americans share?

Every culture has its own traditions. Games and sports are part of these traditions. So are arts, such as music and dance. Other traditions can involve wearing certain clothes or doing other special things.

Many of our sports began as traditions in certain cultures. Do you like to play soccer? This sport came to us from Europe. So did golf, skiing, and ice-skating. Surfing came from the culture of the Hawaiian Islands.

Our game of soccer comes from England.

Some types of gospel music came from African American music.

We also enjoy gifts from many cultures in our music and other arts. Jazz, rock and roll, and types of gospel music all grew out of African American music. Salsa and tango come from Latino cultures. Japanese Americans share Kabuki, a kind of drama, or play.

Many cultures have their own dances. Do you know how to clog? Clogging was started in the United States by people from Ireland, Scotland, and other countries. How about the hula? This style of dancing comes to us from Hawaii.

What are some traditions that people share where you live? What are some favorite traditions in your family?

6. Our Community Expresses Itself

People take pride in expressing their culture. Two ways that they do this is through writing and artwork. Many artists and writers show their cultural backgrounds in their work.

Kadir Nelson is an African American artist. His paintings are of African American culture. Some of his work shows famous African Americans. Others shows those who are struggling.

Tomie dePaola is a writer of Italian and Irish heritage. He wrote children's books. His most famous book is *Strega Nona*. In the story, Strega Nona is an Italian woman who makes pasta. Strega is from the same place as dePaola's ancestors who came to America.

Kadir Nelson's paintings focus on African American culture.

Amy Tan wrote *The Joy Luck Club*. The characters in the book have the same cultural background as Tan.

Carmen Lomas Garza is a Mexican American artist. Garza painted the beauty in everyday Mexican American life. One of her paintings shows a birthday celebration with people dancing and talking. There is even a piñata. Celebrations are an important part of Mexican American culture.

Amy Tan is an Asian American writer. Tan is part of a Chinese immigrant family. Her most famous book, *The Joy Luck Club,* is about Chinese immigrants. The book follows four mothers and daughters in immigrant families. The story describes their experiences as immigrants in the United States.

These people create these works for different reasons. Sometimes they just want to express their backgrounds. Others find that their culture brings out their best work. And others do it to inform others and bring change.

Hands-On Activity Notes

Activity Online

Write down unique cultural items that start with the correct letter until you run out of time!

Round 1	Round 2
Cultural Items That Start with the Letter ______	Cultural Items That Start with the Letter ______
______ ☐	______ ☐
______ ☐	______ ☐
______ ☐	______ ☐
______ ☐	______ ☐
______ ☐	______ ☐
______ ☐	______ ☐
______ ☐	______ ☐
______ ☐	______ ☐
______ ☐	______ ☐
______ ☐	______ ☐
______ ☐	______ ☐
______ ☐	______ ☐
______ ☐	______ ☐
Points (count all items that do NOT have an X): ☐	Points (count all items that do NOT have an X): ☐

Round 3

Cultural Items That Start with the Letter ______

______ ☐
______ ☐
______ ☐
______ ☐
______ ☐
______ ☐
______ ☐
______ ☐
______ ☐
______ ☐
______ ☐
______ ☐
______ ☐

Points (count all items that do NOT have an X): ☐

Round 4

Cultural Items That Start with the Letter ______

______ ☐
______ ☐
______ ☐
______ ☐
______ ☐
______ ☐
______ ☐
______ ☐
______ ☐
______ ☐
______ ☐
______ ☐
______ ☐

Points (count all items that do NOT have an X): ☐

Summary

Our communities are very diverse. People in our country have come from around the world. With them, they have brought cultures that influence American culture.

You see how diverse American culture is by studying the community around you. You see it in the foods we eat and in the languages we speak. You can see it in our holidays and in our traditions. Does our diverse country make your life more interesting? What do you think?

Show What You Know

Think of something in your community that comes from a certain culture. Try to choose something you can find or make so you can share it with the class.

- Name of the item: ____________________
- Cultural category or categories (foods, languages, holidays, traditions, arts):

  ____
- Culture the item comes from: ____________________
- Something interesting about the item, such as how it is made or what it is used for:

  ____

  ____

  ____

  ____

Lesson 7

Making Communities Better

How do people improve their communities?

Introduction

Our communities bring us many good things. They are full of diverse people and interesting places. But communities have problems, too. When people see these problems, they can help solve them. Every person has a chance to improve their community. Just one person can make a big difference.

In this lesson, you will learn why helping to improve your community is an important part of being a good citizen. You will learn how improving your community benefits everyone who lives in it.

You will also read about six people who set out to solve problems in their own communities. Other people did not always like what these six people did at first. But in the end, these people each made their community a better place to live. Their work also helped people in many other places. What problems do you see in your community?

Vocabulary

boycott
citizenship
common good
disabilities
strike

These kids are cleaning up their local park. By cleaning up the park, they are improving their community.

1. Good Citizens Help Their Community

To be a good citizen, you should treat your classmates with respect.

You are part of a community in the United States. It is important that you help out your community. This is part of good **citizenship**. All people in our country should practice good citizenship.

There are many things you can do every day to be a good citizen. You should treat everyone around you with respect. No matter how they look or act, all your classmates are equals. You must treat them this way at all times.

The United States has laws that you have to follow. These laws tell you that you cannot steal or try to hurt other people. If you see someone breaking a law, it is your job either to stop them or to tell someone else.

As you grow older, you will gain more responsibilities. One day, you may have a family to support. For this reason, you should work hard in school. When you get a job, you should do your best at it. One day, you will also be old enough to vote. Voting is another way to contribute to the community.

You should do your part in keeping the **common good**. The common good is what is best for everyone in your community. Keeping your community clean is one example of contributing to the common good. When someone litters, everyone is affected.

These are some of the things that all people of the United States have a responsibility to do. But some people go above and beyond these duties to make their community a better place. You will read about six people who practiced excellent citizenship.

Volunteering is one way to practice good citizenship. These people are helping their community by building a house.

Preview Activity

Listen carefully to the story about Rosa Parks.

Think of words that could go on a plaque for the Rosa Parks monument. Write them in the spaces below.

Rosa Parks

What did she do to improve her community?

___

___

When did she do this?

___

In what ways was she a good citizen?

___

___

Vocabulary Activity

Activity Online

Read the plaque below that describes a good citizen. Then fill in the correct terms.

Vocabulary Word Bank

boycott
citizenship
common good
disabilities
strike

A Good Citizen

A good citizen takes their ______________ seriously. Good citizens work for the ______________, not just for themselves or people that look like them. They work to make sure everyone is treated equally and with respect.

When good citizens notice something unfair in their community, they take action. They might choose to organize a ______________ or ______________ to bring attention to their cause. Anyone can be a good citizen, no matter their age, gender, ______________, or beliefs.

Hands-On Activity

Activity Online

Create human monuments honoring the contributions of six individuals whose actions made a difference in the lives of people in their own community and around the country.

Directions: Creating Human Monuments

1. **Read your assigned section to learn about a good citizen who helped their community.** Your group will be assigned one of six historical people. In your Activity Notes, complete the row about your person. (You will fill out the rows about the other people later.)
2. **Work with your group to plan a human monument for your person.** With your group, complete the steps as described in your Activity Notes. When you finish each step, get your teacher's initials before moving to the next step.
   - **Step 1:** Assign the four jobs.
   - **Step 2:** Talk about who each group member will be in the monument.
   - **Step 3:** Design the monument.
   - **Step 4:** Write a plaque for the monument.
   - **Step 5:** Decide the location for the monument.
   - **Step 6:** Prepare to present the monument.
   - **Step 7:** Take a photograph of your monument.

Clara Barton helped many different people during her life.

2. Clara Barton Helps Soldiers

From early in her life, Clara Barton wanted to help others. When her brother suffered a severe injury after falling from a roof, she cared for him. In 1838, when she was a teenager, Barton began teaching at a schoolhouse in her hometown of North Oxford, Massachusetts.

Most teachers at this time were men, but Barton was very good at teaching. She opened a free school so that kids who could not afford other schools could get an education. Within one year, the school grew to 600 students under Barton's direction. But because she was a woman, the school board did not hire her as the head of the school.

This did not lessen Barton's desire to help people. When the Civil War began, Barton was able to assist. Her father had been part of the military and had encouraged her to care for soldiers during the war.

At first, she gathered medical supplies and treated soldiers returning from the battlefield. But she really wanted to be on the front lines. Very few women went near the battlefields, but this did not stop Barton.

When she got there, she did whatever she could to help out. She cleaned hospitals, cared for soldiers, and even risked her life coming to the aid of wounded soldiers. Soldiers called her the "Angel of the Battlefield."

After the war, Barton continued her service to the communities around her. She founded the American Red Cross, which helped people after disasters like floods or fires. Barton was the organization's first president. You may have heard of the Red Cross. That's because the American Red Cross continues to help people all over the country.

Thanks to Barton, people can get help from the American Red Cross after a natural disaster. The people here are getting supplies after an earthquake.

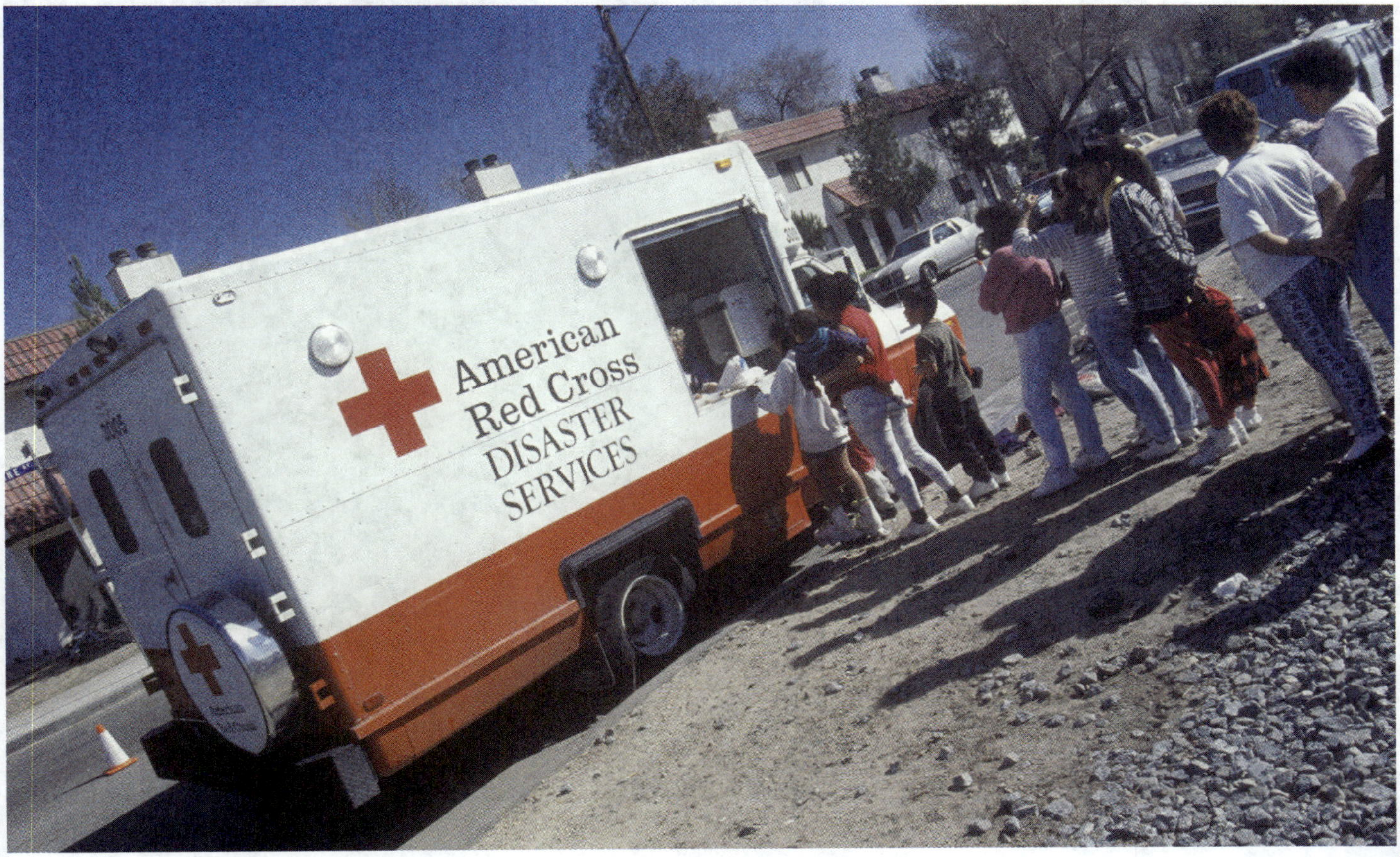

3. César Chávez Helps Farmworkers

César (SAY-zahr) Chávez was born near Yuma, Arizona, and came from a poor family. When he was still young, César and his family moved to California. As a teenager, he became a migrant farmworker to help his family.

Migrant farmworkers often had hard lives. They worked long hours for very little pay. Often, workers got sick or hurt because they had to use unsafe chemicals and machines. César and his family also faced many hardships as farmworkers.

César Chávez made life better for farmworkers.

As a young man, César wanted to help the farmworkers. In 1962, he helped to start a new group that became known as the United Farm Workers of America, or UFW. The UFW helped farmworkers ask for better pay and safer working conditions.

At that time, César lived in the town of Delano, California. There were farms all around the town. At first, the farm owners there refused to listen to the UFW. So, César told all the workers to stop picking the crops. Stopping work in this way is called a **strike**. César hoped the strike would make the owners pay more attention to the workers.

These people are marching to show their support for the UFW.

The owners still did not listen. César took another step. He asked people to stop buying what the farms sold. This is called a **boycott**.

It took César and the UFW five years, but many of the farm owners finally gave in. They agreed to pay the farmworkers more and also promised to make the work safer.

César Chávez helped to make Delano a better place for farmworkers. He went on to help farmworkers in many other places around the country for the next 30 years. César helped them get better pay and safer working conditions.

4. Ruby Bridges Helps African Americans

In 1960, Ruby Bridges was six years old and ready to start first grade. When she did, she would make history.

Ruby lived in New Orleans, Louisiana. At that time, Black students and White students in New Orleans went to different schools. Ruby would be the first African American to go to the White school near her home.

Many White people were upset. They wanted Black and White students to be kept apart. Still, Ruby's mother was hopeful. She thought the school was a good one. And she thought that it was time that Black and White children went to the same schools. But Ruby's father was worried. "We're just asking for trouble," he said.

Ruby Bridges made history when she was just six years old.

Ruby's first day of school was frightening. Outside the school, crowds of angry people threw things at her and yelled that Black children did not belong in their schools. Ruby thought some of them might even hurt her.

Inside the school, Ruby discovered that she was the only student in her classroom. All the others had stayed home.

For months, Ruby was the only student in her class. Still, she kept coming to school. People started to see that she was not going away. When she returned to school the next year, many students had returned to their classes.

Ruby made it easier for all children in New Orleans to go to good schools together. As an adult, Ruby helps people in other communities, too. She talks to children and adults about her experience and how we can still learn from it today.

Ruby helped to show people that Black and White children could go to the same schools.

5. Lois Marie Gibbs Helps Make Her Community Safer

In 1978, Lois Marie Gibbs lived in Niagara Falls, New York. Lois had two children, Michael and Melissa. Michael became very sick. Lois wanted to know why.

There was an old canal, or waterway, near Michael's school called Love Canal. Businesses had been dumping dangerous chemicals into the canal for years before it was buried in the ground.

The school playground was built where the canal used to be. Lois thought chemicals in the old canal were making her son sick. Lois did not know what to do. No one believed her fears about Love Canal.

Lois asked her neighbors about their health. It turned out that many of the children in the area were sick. Some scientists agreed that the canal could be the problem.

Lois decided to do something about it. She got all her neighbors together. Lois and her neighbors knew they needed help. They decided to tell everyone they could about their problem.

Lois Gibbs wanted to know why children near Love Canal were getting sick.

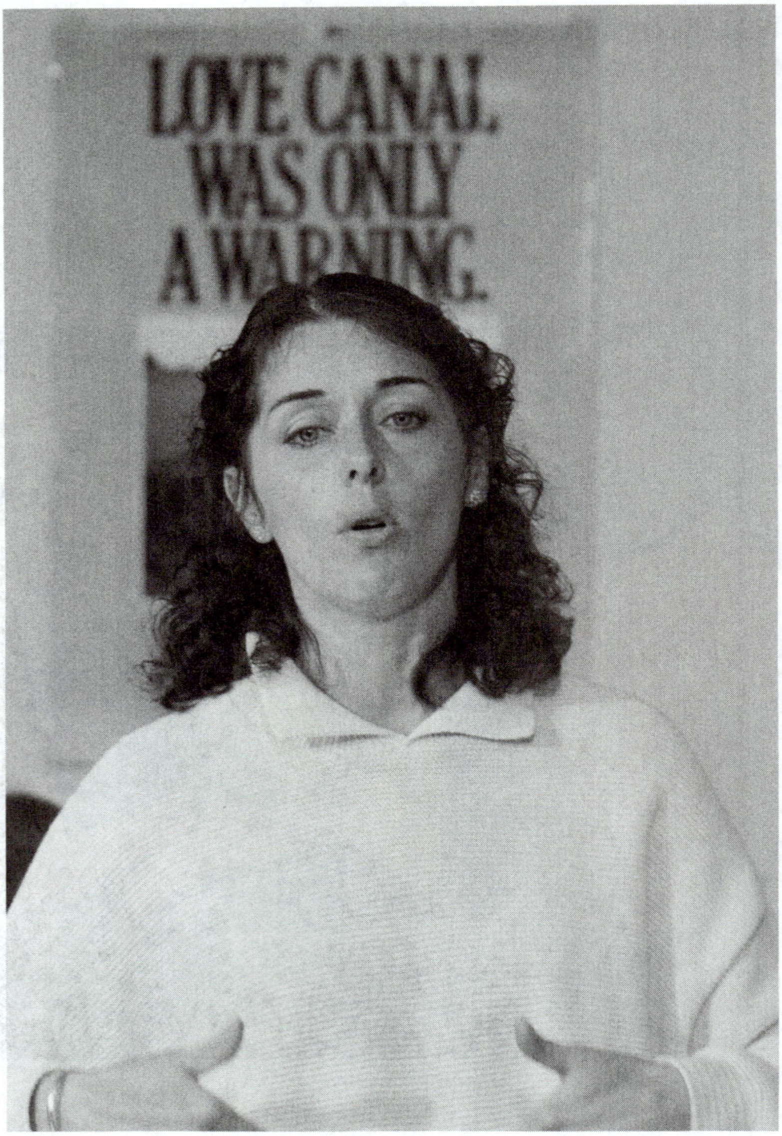

This school was closed because of the chemicals in Love Canal.

Lois and her neighbors made signs to carry and held protests. Then they followed the governor of New York around. People saw them on television.

Finally, the governor came to visit Love Canal. He agreed to help families move to a safer place. Later, President Jimmy Carter helped, too. The school was closed. It was torn down, along with hundreds of homes. The government helped people move to new homes.

Lois Gibbs made a big difference in her community. Later, she helped people in other towns and cities. She showed them how to join together to make their communities safe places to live in.

6. Judy Heumann Helps People With Disabilities

Judy Heumann (HEW-man) was born in 1947. When she was a baby, she got sick with polio. This disease hurt her legs. Judy would never be able to walk. She had to use a wheelchair to get around.

Judy lived in Brooklyn, New York. On her first day of first grade, her mother brought her to school. The principal would not let Judy in because she used a wheelchair. A teacher came to Judy's house for a few hours each week instead.

When Judy was in fourth grade, she was finally allowed to go to school. There, she met other people with **disabilities**. Someone with a disability has a physical or mental condition that limits their daily life activities. Judy learned that other students with disabilities felt the same way she did. She could not use her legs, but she wanted to learn as much as any other student.

In college, Judy studied to be a teacher. At first, New York City would not let her teach because she used a wheelchair. Judy went to court to win the right to teach. When the city realized it would lose in court, it let Judy teach.

Judy Heumann started the group Disabled in Action.

In 1970, Judy formed a group called Disabled in Action. She started the group to protect people with disabilities in New York from being treated unfairly. The group has grown a lot since then. It helps people with disabilities all across the country to live better lives.

After creating Disabled in Action, Judy worked closely with the government of the United States. She helped to make sure that people with disabilities have the same rights as everyone else under the law. She continues today to fight for the rights of people with disabilities.

Thanks to Judy, disabled students are treated more fairly.

7. Billy Frank Jr. Helps Native Americans

Billy Frank Jr. was born in 1931 in Washington. He was a member of the Nisqually tribe. Growing up, he learned to fish in local rivers.

When Frank was 14 years old, he went to the Nisqually River to fish for salmon. However, two state officials came to arrest him. They believed he was breaking a Washington state law that banned fishing.

Frank believed his arrest was unfair. Although the law banned fishing, there was a treaty in place that said local Native American groups had the right to fish in Washington. A treaty is an official agreement. This treaty was made a long time ago and recognized by the U.S. government.

Frank felt that the state did not respect tribal rights or the environment. Fishing was an important tradition to Native American groups in the area. It also helps to maintain a healthy ecosystem for the river.

Billy Frank Jr. talks about the importance of preserving Puget Sound, an important marine environment.

The Billy Frank Jr. Nisqually National Wildlife Refuge helps to preserve nature and wildlife around the Nisqually River Delta.

For many years, Frank fought to protect tribal rights. He gathered supporters and organized demonstrations to make his voice heard. He wanted Washington to recognize that Native Americans have a right to help protect natural resources in the state.

Finally in 1974, Frank's efforts paid off. A federal court sided with Native American groups in the case *United States v. Washington*. The court said that Native Americans have the right to fish. The court also said that tribes should work with Washington state to manage the salmon resource.

Frank kept fighting to protect tribal rights and the environment. He and other activists worked closely with the government to preserve nature.

Frank passed away in 2014, but his story lives on. In 2015, President Barack Obama recognized Frank's work and awarded him the Presidential Medal of Freedom. Today, you can visit the Billy Frank Jr. Nisqually National Wildlife Refuge in Washington.

Hands-On Activity Notes

How were these people good citizens? List at least two ways each person helped his or her community. Take additional notes on how this person was a good citizen.

Person		**How They Helped Their Community**
	Clara Barton (Section 2)	
	César Chávez (Section 3)	
	Ruby Bridges (Section 4)	
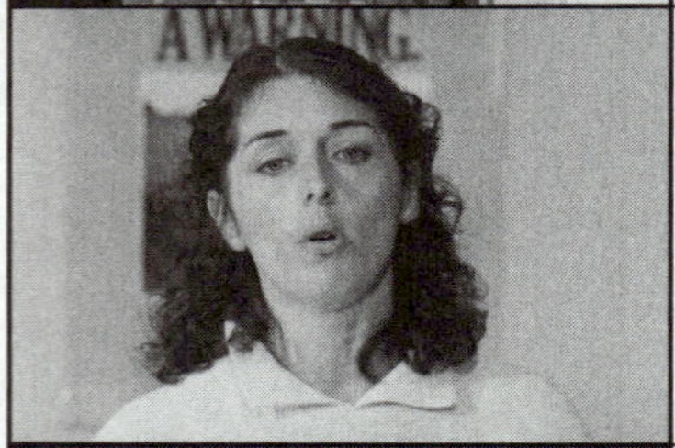	Lois Marie Gibbs (Section 5)	
	Judy Heumann (Section 6)	
	Billy Frank Jr. (Section 7)	

Activity Online

How They Were a Good Citizen

Steps for Creating a Human Monument

Record the name of the person you read about. Then, follow the steps to create a human monument with your group.

____

______ **Step 1: Assign the four roles.**

Each member of your group will have one of four roles: Speaker, Sculptor, Writer, or Geographer.

______________ will be the Speaker.

______________ will be the Sculptor.

______________ will be the Writer.

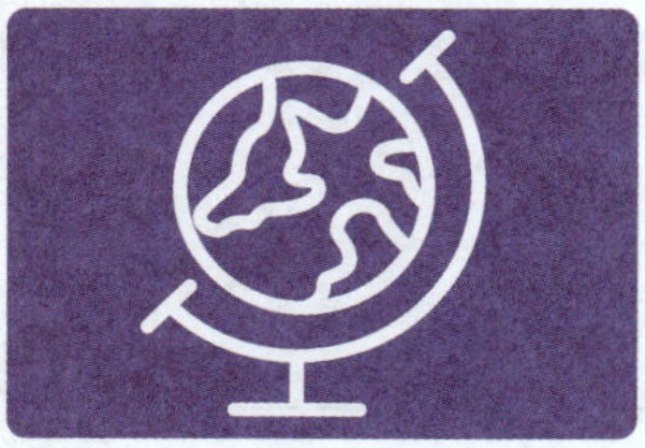

______________ will be the Geographer.

_____ Step 2: Talk about who each group member will be in the monument.

Talk about the role each of you will have in the monument. The Speaker leads the discussion and takes notes below.

Name of Group Member	Who or what will this group member represent in the monument?	How will this group member pose in the monument?

_____ Step 3: Design the monument.

Talk about what the monument will look like. Brainstorm ideas for four props to use. The Sculptor leads this discussion. The Sculptor also assigns each group member to bring one of the props.

Prop	Group Member Who Will Bring the Prop

Now practice getting in position for the monument. The Sculptor leads the practice. Practice until you are happy with the design.

Step 4: Write a plaque for the monument.

Talk about a sentence to put on a plaque for your monument. The sentence should tell what the person did to improve the community. The Writer leads this discussion.

The Writer writes a first draft of the sentence in the space below. As a group, check the draft. Make sure it is written neatly. Check that all the words are spelled correctly. The Writer makes any corrections that are needed.

_____ Step 5: Decide the location for the monument.

Talk about where to put your monument. Which community on the map should it go in? The Geographer leads this discussion and writes the group's answers below.

Name of community: ______________________________

Our monument should go here because ______________________________

____

____

Circle the name of the community on the map below.

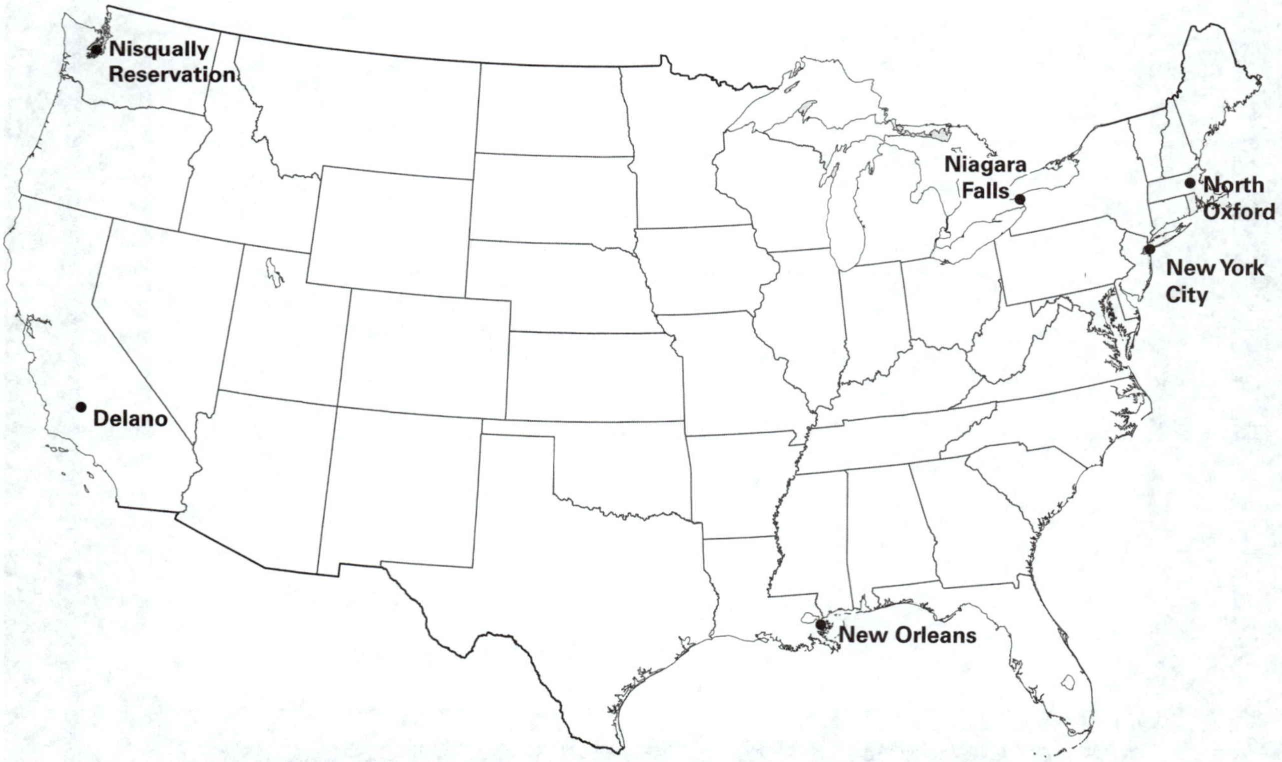

______ **Step 6: Prepare to present the monument.**

Rehearse presenting your monument.

- ☐ The Sculptor leads the rehearsal. The Sculptor also makes sure that each group member has brought a prop. As a group, practice getting into position and holding the position for two minutes. The Sculptor practices thanking the audience in a loud, clear voice. The Sculptor brings a prop for the monument.

- ☐ The Speaker practices telling who each group member is in the monument and what he or she is doing. The Speaker talks in a loud, clear voice. The Speaker brings a prop for the monument.

- ☐ The Writer neatly copies the plaque onto a new sheet of paper. Be sure to write in large letters and spell all words correctly. The Writer practices reading the plaque in a loud, clear voice. The Writer brings a prop for the monument.

- ☐ The Geographer practices telling where the monument will be placed and why. The Geographer speaks in a loud, clear voice. The Geographer brings a prop for the monument.

______ **Step 7: Take a photograph of your monument.**

Take a picture of your human monument. Make sure the photo includes all group members, props, and the plaque.

Summary

In this lesson, you learned ways to practice good citizenship. You also met six people who showed how to be good citizens. Clara Barton, César Chávez, Ruby Bridges, Lois Marie Gibbs, Judy Heumann, and Billy Frank Jr. all helped to improve their communities. They made the lives of the people around them better. Their work helped people in many other places, too.

You, too, can make a difference in your community. There are things that you can do every day to lend a hand. What can you think of doing to make your community a better place?

Show What You Know

Identify someone who has made a difference in your community. Write a plaque to tell what this good citizen did. Use complete sentences.

Lesson 8

Cultures Around the World

How are people around the world alike and different?

Introduction

You and your friends probably do many of the same things every day. But your life may have been very different if you had been born in another country. What do you think children in other parts of the world do?

Some things are the same no matter where we live. Everyone eats and sleeps. Nearly all children play. In most places, children also go to school. But they do not all do these things in exactly the same way. In fact, in some places, children's lives are very different from yours.

In this lesson, you will read about the lives of children in six different countries. As you read, think about how each child's day is like yours and how it is different.

Vocabulary

environment

Children from different places may have different ways of life. But many children around the world go to school every day just like you.

London has things that are similar to and different from American cities. One difference is that people drive cars in London on the left side of the road instead of the right side.

1. Cultures in Different Countries

You are very familiar with the way you and your family live. But how do people in other parts of the world live? Do you think their lives are similar to or different from yours?

Different cultures affect how people live. Culture is made up of different things. Food, clothes, and everyday activities are all parts of culture. However, what people eat, wear, and do each day change from place to place.

Some countries have cultures that are very similar to U.S. culture, but others have cultures that are different. If you visit a city in Canada, it might look similar to a city in the United States. If you went to a city in India, however, it might look very different.

The **environment** can influence a country's culture. For example, rice is a common food in many countries in Asia. This is because the wet climate there is ideal for growing rice.

The environment can also affect the clothes people wear. In warm places like countries in central Africa, people tend to wear lighter clothing. In colder places like northern Russia, they need heavier clothes to stay warm.

The environment also affects where people live. For example, the country of Japan is an island with many mountains inland. It is hard to build homes on the mountains, so few people live inland. Instead, most people live in cities along the coast, where land is flatter. Also, the ocean provides food and transportation for the people living near it.

As you read, think about how the environment has affected culture in each country. How does it compare to culture in America?

Many parts of Asia have a wet climate, which is ideal for growing rice. This is why rice is such an important part of the culture in these countries.

Preview Activity

Activity Online

Think about the environment in which you live. List five things that affect your everyday activities, the way you dress, and what you eat.

1. ______________________________

2. ______________________________

3. ______________________________

4. ______________________________

5. ______________________________

What decisions have you made today because of the environment in which you live? Draw a picture of one of those decisions.

Vocabulary Activity

Activity Online

Draw three different **environments**, and show and label how each might affect the way you eat, dress, or live.

Hands-On Activity

With a partner, travel around the world to meet students like you from six different cultures. Then share what you have learned with the class.

Directions: Visiting a Culture Around the World

1. **Start by reviewing the six continents where the students you will visit live.**
2. **Meet and greet your partner.** Describe three favorite parts of your culture.
3. **Collect your materials.** You will need drawing and coloring supplies to complete your Activity Notes.
4. **Pick a cultural station to visit.** With your partner, agree on a cultural station to learn more about.
5. **Read the text section that corresponds to your cultural station.**
6. **Complete your Activity Notes for your cultural station.**
7. **Show your work to your teacher.**

Directions: Sharing Cultures

1. **With your partner, pick one student and his or her culture to share with the class.**
2. **Collect the student statuette and Cultural Mysteries cards for your culture.**
3. **Share what you have learned about your student's culture.** Use your completed Activity Notes to help you.
4. **If you are not presenting, complete the Activity Notes for any remaining cultural stations.** Listen carefully as other pairs present what they have learned.

2. Josie Lives in Canada

Josie lives in a small town in northern Canada. Josie's family is Inuit (IH-noo-wet). The Inuit people have lived in Canada for 3,000 years or more.

It is cold and snowy most of the year where Josie lives. Josie skis to school. Her best friend, Ivy, rides to school on a snowmobile. At school, they eat a hot breakfast.

Josie is learning to use a computer at school. Her other classes are reading, math, and history. Josie does not speak English. She speaks Inuktitut (ih-NOOK-teh-toot) with her family and friends.

On weekends, Josie's family sometimes goes ice fishing. They make holes in the ice and try to catch fish in the water below. Josie also likes to play in the snow with her dog, Max.

Josie's family goes ice fishing on the weekends.

Josie lives in the northern part of Canada.

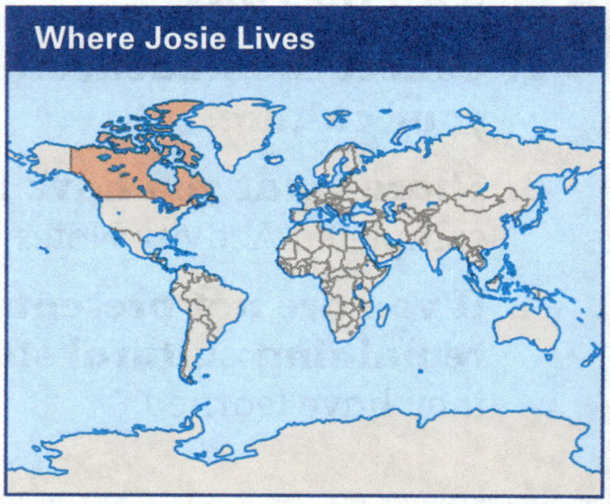

One of Josie's favorite meals is caribou stew. Caribou are large deer that live in Josie's part of the world.

Josie's warmest boots are handmade from sealskin. Some of her blankets are made of sealskin, too. Josie, Ivy, and their friends use the blankets to play a blanket toss game. Lots of people play together. Several people hold the edges of the sealskin blanket. One person stands in the middle of the blanket, and the others toss him or her into the air. Josie and Ivy both love to bounce on the blanket.

Josie and her friends like to play blanket toss.

Hands-On Activity Notes

Activity Online

Complete each box.

Geography

Color and label the country Josie lives in.

Cultural Mystery 1

Make a quick drawing of the photograph and show what might come out of the hole.

Cultural Mystery 2

What is special about how Josie's boots are made?

____

____

____

3. Luis Lives in Paraguay

Luis lives on a farm in a country in South America called Paraguay. He lives with his mother, father, and three brothers.

Luis wakes up before sunrise every morning so he can help his father and brothers in the fields. There is always something to be done on the farm. Luis might plant seeds, hoe weeds, or pick crops.

Luis and his family often take a break to drink terere (teh-reh-REH). Terere is made in a cup with water and dried, crushed leaves. The cup is called a guampa (WAHM-pah). The guampa is usually made from a cow's horn. Luis sips the drink through a metal straw. The straw has a strainer at one end to keep out the leaves.

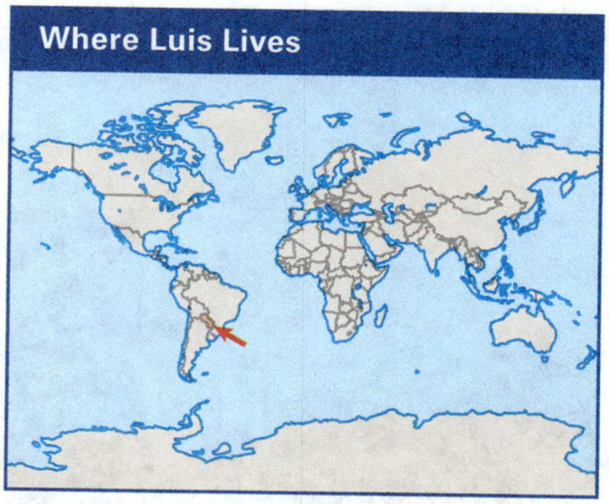

Luis lives on a farm in Paraguay.

Luis's father works hard in the fields.

Luis and his brother ride their horse to school five days a week.

Luis goes to school five days a week. He and his brother Esteban (es-TAY-bahn) ride their family's horse to school, which is several miles from their farm.

Luis's favorite part of school is playing with his friends. During breaks, they play soccer. They call the game fútbol (FOOT-bohl).

Most of Luis's classes are in Spanish. However, outside of class, Luis and his friends like to speak Guarani (gwahr-uh-NEE). Guarani is a language that people in Paraguay have spoken for hundreds of years. Luis likes the fact that people still speak Guarani today.

Hands-On Activity Notes

Complete each box.

Activity Online

Geography

Color and label the country Luis lives in.

Cultural Mystery 1

Sketch the cup and straw Luis uses to drink terere. Next to your drawing, write the name of the special cup.

Cultural Mystery 2

What language other than Spanish do many people in Paraguay speak? Why does Luis like speaking it?

4. Kazuo Lives in Japan

Kazuo and his family put away their blankets and futons every morning.

Kazuo (KAH-zoo-oh) lives in Tokyo (TOH-kee-OH). Tokyo is a large city by the ocean in the country of Japan.

Each morning, Kazuo wakes up in the room he shares with his little brother. The rooms in Kazuo's house are small because many people live in Tokyo, and housing there is expensive.

Kazuo's room has sliding doors made of paper. These doors are called shoji (shoh-gee). Kazuo and the rest of his family sleep on thick mattresses called futons. Each morning, they roll up their futons and blankets and put them in the closet.

For breakfast, Kazuo and his brother eat cereal. His parents eat rice and egg with chopsticks.

Kazuo's parents start the day with egg on rice, a popular Japanese breakfast.

After breakfast, Kazuo's father hurries to catch the train to work. Kazuo's mother stays home to take care of his little brother.

Meanwhile, Kazuo gets ready for school. After he gets his schoolbag, he goes to the front door to put on his shoes. Kazuo's family members never wear shoes in the house.

Kazuo goes to school six days a week. He rides the bus with his friends. They all wear navy blue uniforms. Kazuo speaks Japanese with his friends, but in school he is studying English.

Kazuo and his friends practice a sport called kendo (ken-doh) in gym class. In kendo, they use bamboo sticks like swords. They put on face masks and gloves so they do not get hurt.

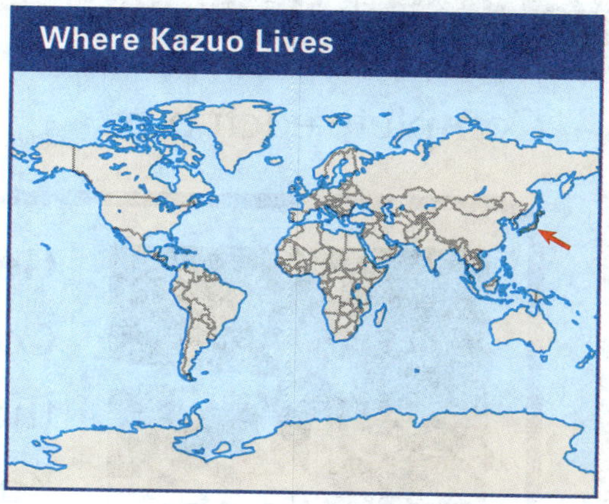

Kazuo lives by the coast in Japan.

Kazuo and his friends practice kendo for fun.

Activity Online

Complete each box.

Geography

Color and label the country Kazuo lives in.

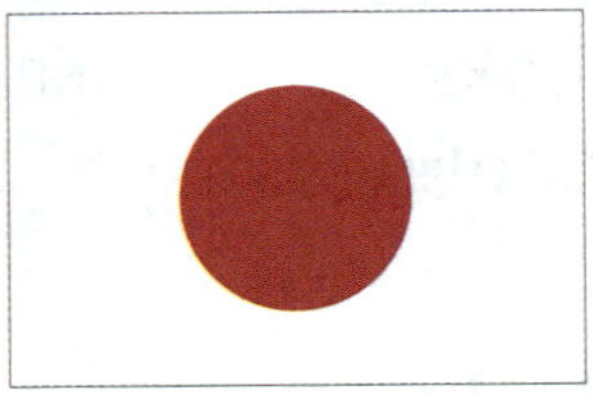

Cultural Mystery 1

How is Kazuo's home different from your home?

Cultural Mystery 2

Draw the mask Kazuo wears when he practices Kendo.

5. Emma Lives in Hungary

Emma lives in a small city in Hungary, a country in central Europe. Emma lives in an old house with her mother and two brothers.

Every morning, Emma feeds the geese in the backyard. Then she eats breakfast before walking to school with her brothers, Viktor and Sandor (SHAN-dor).

Emma is in third grade. Her favorite class is music. All students in Hungary must learn a foreign language. Emma is learning French. However, she speaks Hungarian with her friends.

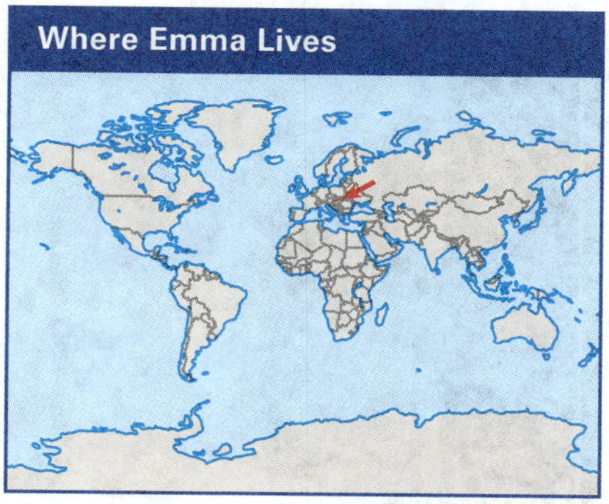

Emma lives in a small city in Hungary.

Emma feeds her geese every morning before school.

Emma likes to show her skill on the parallel bars.

Emma and her brothers are good at sports. Viktor plays soccer. Sandor is on the school's swim team. Their school has an indoor swimming pool. Emma practices gymnastics in school twice a week. Her favorite thing to do in gymnastics is the parallel bars.

Emma has music lessons on Tuesday afternoons. She is learning to play the flute. Her mother thinks Emma plays beautiful music. But her brothers cover their ears when she plays. Someday, Emma wants to play the flute in an orchestra like her uncle Zoltan (ZOHL-tahn).

Hands-On Activity Notes

Activity Online

Complete each box.

Geography

Color and label the country Emma lives in.

Cultural Mystery 1

What is Emma's dream to do one day?

Cultural Mystery 2

Draw Emma practicing her favorite thing to do in gymnastics.

6. Paul Lives in Australia

Paul and his family raise cattle on their ranch.

Paul lives on a cattle ranch in the country of Australia. The cattle ranch is far from any city or town. Australians call areas of their country like this the outback. It is hot and dusty where Paul lives in the outback.

When Paul gets up in the morning, he puts on a T-shirt and jeans. Then he puts on tall leather boots. He wears a hat to keep the sun off his neck.

Paul eats eggs and snags, or sausages, for breakfast. After breakfast, Paul takes care of his horse, Scout. Later in the day, he will ride out with his father to check on the cattle.

Paul and his two sisters go to school for an hour and a half a day. Actually, they don't go to school—school comes to them!

Paul lives on a ranch in Australia.

Where Paul Lives

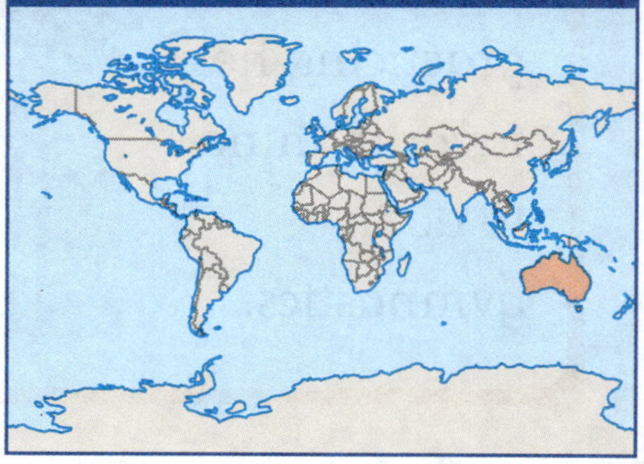

The school is called Schools of the Air. There are not enough students near Paul for a school. Therefore, Paul and his sisters go to school online everyday. Paul spends his school day doing lessons. Then he does his homework.

Paul would rather be eating a sandwich than doing homework. Paul spreads butter and a brown paste made from yeast extract and vegetables on bread or crackers. It is his favorite snack.

Once a week, Paul's family drives to the store in town. Sometimes, they stop at another ranch to see if their friends need anything. Paul's friend, Gary, lives on this ranch. Paul and Gary like to play video games and ride their horses.

Paul goes to school through a computer.

Hands-On Activity Notes

Activity Online

Complete each box.

Geography

Color and label the country Paul lives in.

Cultural Mystery 1

What is Paul's favorite snack and what is it made from?

____

____

Cultural Mystery 2

Draw a picture of Paul's family ranch and what they raise there.

7. Miriam Lives in Nigeria

Miriam lives in a town in Nigeria, a country in Africa. Miriam has 11 brothers and sisters. She helps look after the younger ones. She likes to use her doll to play-act stories for them.

Miriam likes school. She does well in math and geography. She also studies history and health.

Everyone speaks English at school. Miriam also speaks Hausa (HOW-seh). Hausa is one of hundreds of languages in Nigeria.

After school, Miriam watches television. Then she does her homework.

After homework, it is time for dinner. Food in Nigeria can be very spicy. People often cook with hot peppers. Miriam eats a lot of rice, beans, corn, and yams. She also eats fruit every day. Mangoes are her favorite.

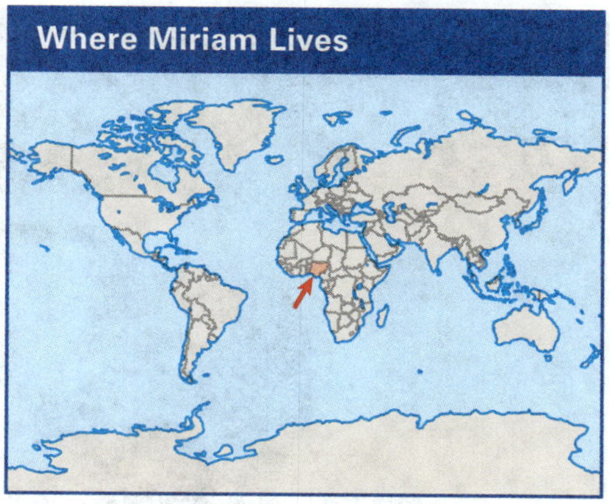

Miriam lives in a town in Nigeria.

Miriam works hard in school.

Drums are an important part of Nigeria's culture.

Miriam also likes a soft drink that is made with ginger. Ginger is the spice used in gingerbread. Miriam likes the taste of ginger.

Miriam is learning to play the drums. "Talking drums" are an important part of juju music. Juju songs tell stories about local people and events. People play juju songs in the evenings. Miriam dances to the music with her friends.

Hands-On Activity Notes

Activity Online

Complete each box.

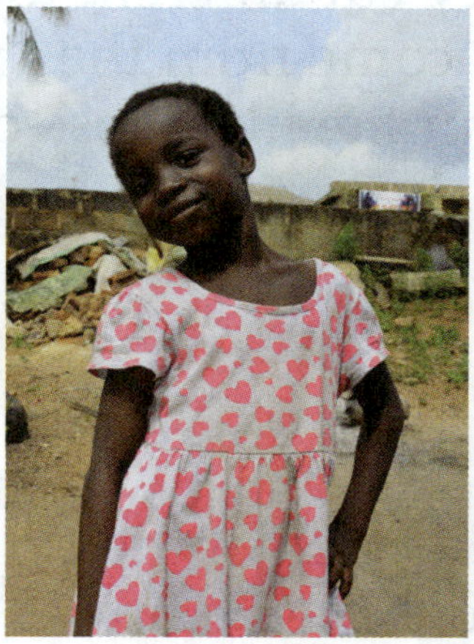

Geography

Color and label the country Miriam lives in.

Cultural Mystery 1

Draw a picture of Miriam playing a drum.

Cultural Mystery 2

In this photograph, we see Miriam's family selling food in front of their home. What are some foods people eat in Nigeria?

Summary

You have just read about children in six places around the world. In many ways, their lives are alike. For example, all of them go to school.

But in other ways, their lives are very different. They eat different foods and do different things to have fun. These differences come from the cultures in each country. What about you? How is your life like those of the children you read about? How is it different?

Show What You Know

Choose two students you learned about and describe each of their environments. Write something you appreciate about their culture.

Josie Lives in Canada

Luis Lives in Paraguay

Kazuo Lives in Japan

Emma Lives in Hungary

Paul Lives in Australia

Miriam Lives in Nigeria

Student	His or Her Environment	Something You Appreciate

Unit 3

Economics

Bring economic images to life and then ask your own questions about the economy. Experience being a buyer and seller in a marketplace. Debate real-life economic situations and play a game to test your budgeting skills. Take on the role of countries conducting trade around the world. Conduct an inquiry to explore the role of scarcity in the world around us.

Unit Inquiry Project

1 Gathering Visual Evidence

What has happened to this boat?	
What do you think might be in the containers? Why? (Each container is 8 feet wide, 20 feet long, and 9 feet high!)	
There are other boats waiting for this boat to get unstuck. Why is this a bad thing for people wanting to sell the goods on those other boats?	

2 Developing the Compelling Question

Unit Storyline

The Ever Given is a large container ship. A container ship moves goods from one place to another so that those goods can be sold. This ship is 1,312 feet long and 192 feet wide. It can carry 20,124 containers when fully loaded. In 2021, this ship was stuck in the Suez Canal in Egypt for six days. No other ships were able to make it through the canal. It is estimated that the world economy lost $400 million every hour that the ship was stuck. Without goods, like coffee, being able to make it to market, the cost went up. Why does this happen? How do events like this affect the choices people make?

Unit Compelling Question

How are choices people make affected by available resources?

List three questions you have about the Unit Storyline and Compelling Question.

1.

2.

3.

3 Collecting Evidence

After you complete each lesson, return to this table and answer the questions. You will be gathering key information that will help you complete the Unit Inquiry Project.

Lesson	Supporting Questions	What I Learned
9 Understanding Our Economy	How does a free market economy work? Describe two goods and two services that you have bought or used recently.	
10 Choices in a Free Market	What factors can make the price of a good go up or down? What is an economic choice that you have made lately?	
11 Using Money Wisely	Why do people and businesses save money? What are some ways that you or your family can save or invest?	
12 The United States and Global Trade	Why and what do countries trade? List one way that global trade affects you. List one way it affects other people around the world.	

4 Building Additional Content Knowledge

Gather and evaluate additional sources to answer the Unit Compelling Question: *How are choices people make affected by available resources?*

You may conduct outside research or use these readings from *Social Studies Alive! Our Community and Beyond* Social Studies Stories:

- Becoming an Entrepreneur
- Creating a Budget
- How Trade is Changing Bengaluru

Source Title(s)	
Additional Evidence	

5 Constructing an Argument

Write a sentence answering the Unit Compelling Question: *How are choices people make affected by available resources?* This is called a claim.

Then provide at least two pieces of evidence to support your claim. Your evidence can come from the activities you did in class, the readings you completed in your Student Journal or Social Studies Stories, or additional research that you conducted.

Claim:

Evidence:

6 Taking Informed Action

Decide how you want to share what you learned. You could make a poster, a digital presentation, or a video. You might share your presentation with your classmates or with adults in the community.

Lesson 9

Understanding Our Economy

How do we buy and sell things?

Introduction

Have you ever been to a farmers' market? Farmers' markets are places where farmers sell the crops that they grow. People go to these markets so that they can buy different fruits and vegetables that they want.

Sometimes, people buy things from a farmers' market that they can take home, like fruits or vegetables. Other times, people can pay for someone else to do something for them, like paint their faces.

But people cannot buy all of the things that they want. They have to choose between the different things that they want to buy.

How do buyers decide what to buy at a farmers' market? How do sellers try to get people to buy their produce? In this lesson, you'll explore the answers to these questions.

Vocabulary

economy
free market economy
goods
market
scarcity
services

People can buy many different things at a farmers' market. This man is buying vegetables from a seller at the market.

Preview Activity

Activity Online

What is an economy? Make a collage of things that you think are related to our economy.

- Write ECONOMY in large letters in the space below.
- Write words and draw pictures around it.

Vocabulary Activity

Activity Online

Read the story and fill in the blanks with the best vocabulary term. Use each term only once in the story.

Vocabulary Word Bank

~~economy~~ free market economy goods
market scarcity services

A Squirrelly Economy

Andrea, the forgetful squirrel, needs more nuts for the winter! The forest she lives in has a ______________. This means she can buy many different ______________, such as walnuts and acorns, at many different prices.

There are limited amounts of walnuts and acorns. The ______________ of nuts means that prices go up and down sometimes. Andrea forgot to buy acorns! At the ______________, she finds out that acorns are very expensive right now. She doesn't have enough money.

Andrea is known for being a great storyteller that can make anyone laugh. She has an idea! Andrea says, "I know! I'll tell my famous stories in exchange for acorns this fall."

At the market, she offers her ______________ in exchange for acorns. Andrea is happy! She was able to collect enough acorns for the winter and make her friends laugh.

Hands-On Activity

Activity Online

Analyze and ask questions about images related to the economy, and then bring two of the images to life.

Directions: Economic Act-It-Outs

1. **With a partner, carefully analyze a photograph of a market.**
2. **Read the corresponding section of text and write down one question in your Activity Notes.** Is there anything from the reading you want to learn more about?
3. **Work with one other pair, use the Activity Cards to prepare your act-it-out.** Be creative with your answers and your props!
4. **When it is your group's turn, present your act-it-out to the class.** Take turns answering the questions.
5. **Repeat these steps for the remaining images and act-it-outs.**

1. We Buy and Sell Things

Sellers want to sell the food they grow to buyers.

Suppose that you are at a farmers' market with your family. It is early summer. Many farmers have fruits to sell.

Farmers sell different foods that they grow in order to make money. A farmer is a seller at the **market**. A market is any place where buyers and sellers come together to trade.

In a farmers' market, you may notice that there are many different stands selling similar fruits and vegetables. These sellers want buyers to buy from their stand instead of someone else's. In a market, sellers must compete with one another to sell their goods and services to buyers. One way to compete is for sellers to lower the prices of the goods they sell.

Fruits are a popular item at farmers' markets. You may stop and buy different fruits from the stands in the market to take home. When you do this, you are a buyer.

When you choose what fruit to buy, you want to get the best fruit that you can for the lowest price. You may check if the fruit is ripe and not bruised. You may shop around and look at different stands before you decide which fruit you want to buy.

Whenever you buy or sell something, you are part of our **economy**. An economy is made up of all the businesses in a place. Sometimes an economy can be small. The town that the farmers' market is in has an economy. All the businesses in the United States also make up an economy.

Buyers can shop around for things to buy.

2. We Buy Goods and Services

At the farmers' market, people choose to spend their money on many different things. Some choose to spend their money on fruits. Others people may buy popcorn. Some may even pay to get their faces painted.

In an economy, people can choose to spend money on things called **goods** and **services**. Many businesses sell goods. These are items that you can use. There are many different goods that people can buy. Food, clothing, books, and even a house are examples of goods that people spend money on. Usually, a good is something you can touch or see.

When people buy goods, they may use the items just once or many times. The food you buy at the farmers' market is a good that you can use only once. If you buy a toy, you purchase a good that can be used over and over again.

This stuffed animal is a good people can buy.

Going to a petting zoo is a service people can buy.

Some businesses sell services. A service is a task that someone does for you. Some people are paid to cut your hair or even teach you about new things. Unlike goods, you do not keep services that you buy.

People can provide services, such as face painting, at farmers' markets. Some farmers' markets even have petting zoos. There are many animals that you can pet, such as goats and sheep. You could pay a farmer to let you pet and feed the animals. You do not get to keep the animals you pet and feed.

The person who brought the animals to the farmers' market provides a service by bringing the animals and letting you see and pet them. In our economy, people provide many different services for us. Think about services that you and your family use. What are some goods and services that you spend money on?

3. The Things We Buy Are Scarce

When you explore the farmers' market for things to buy, look at how many goods each stand has. One stand may have only a small pile of apples left to sell. Another may have only one jar of honey left. Your family may not be able to buy all the apples or honey that they want.

People want many things. But our wants are always greater than the resources available to produce them. This is called **scarcity**.

Goods and services are scarce. At the farmers' market, each stand can sell different fruits and vegetables. But the farmers who grow the fruit can make only a certain amount each season. Since they can never grow enough fruits and vegetables for everyone to get as much as they want, these goods are scarce.

The amount of food that this girl can buy is limited.

Can your family spend as much time at the farmers' market as they want? There are only 24 hours in a day, and there are even less hours of sunlight. Time, like goods and services, is limited. Because of this, we can say that time is scarce.

When a farmers' market closes, people can no longer shop or spend time there.

If things are scarce, how can we get them? One way that we can get the things we want is by trading for them. But most people get what they want by using money to purchase goods and services. A buyer can buy something with money, and the seller can use this money to buy something else.

Do you have all the money that you want? The answer is probably "no." Because people don't have all the money they want, they must choose between the things they want to buy.

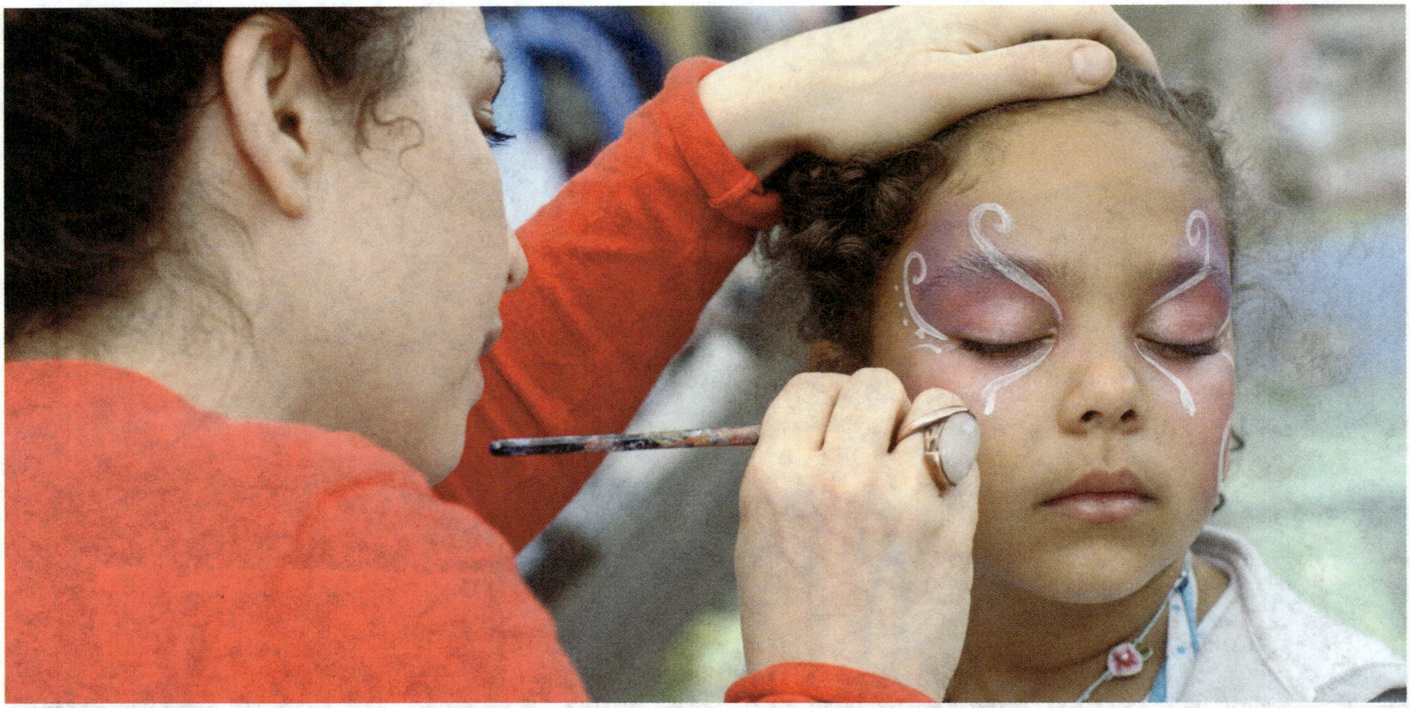

4. There Are Costs and Benefits to What We Buy

You should think about the costs and benefits of getting your face painted before you pay for it.

Buyers do not have enough money to buy everything that they want. They have to choose between the things that they want to have. To make this choice, buyers must think about the benefits and costs of the things they are thinking about buying. A good choice is one in which the benefits are greater than the costs.

While you are at the farmers' market, you may want to get your face painted and also buy a bag of oranges to take home. Both the face painting and oranges cost $4, but you have only $5 to spend. You can choose to buy only the face painting or the bag of oranges.

When you make a choice, you must look at the benefits and costs of each option you have. Each option has some benefits, or things you will gain by choosing it. Each option also has costs, or things you will give up or lose by choosing it.

If you pay to get your face painted, there are costs and benefits. One benefit of getting your face painted is that it is fun to show to other people. One cost of the face painting is that it will last only a day before you have to wash it off, and then your face will not be painted anymore. Another cost is that you will not be able to have fresh oranges with your breakfast!

There are also costs and benefits of buying the oranges. One benefit of the oranges is that they are healthy for you, and you will not be hungry. One cost is that oranges are food, and once you eat them, they are gone. Another cost is that you will not be able to show off your cool face painting!

Looking at the costs and benefits, you may decide that oranges are more important to you. In our economy, people get to make decisions about what they want to buy.

You may buy the bag of oranges after thinking about the benefits.

5. The Free Market Economy

A farmers' market is part of the much larger economy of the United States. The economy of the United States is a **free market economy**. In this type of economy, buyers and sellers make most of the choices.

In some economies, a person, business, or government tells people what to do. In a free market economy, every person is free to make their own choices about what to buy and sell.

Suppose there is a farmer who grows apples. One day, the farmer decides to grow pears instead. The farmer is free to choose to do this.

When the farmer brings those pears to a market, a buyer can choose which fruits or vegetables to buy. The buyer can choose to buy the pears from the farmer. Both the buyer and seller can make their own choices in a free market economy.

This farmer can choose what crops to grow because of the free market economy.

In a free market economy, people are free to choose what jobs they want. Suppose there is a young woman who works on a farm. She might help to grow food for a farmer to sell at a farmers' market. She could choose to quit her job and study to become a doctor or a scientist. She could also choose to start her own farm and grow crops to sell.

Because sellers can make choices in a free market economy, they can sell many different types of goods and services. Buyers then have more choices of what to buy.

In a free market economy, people can choose what they want to do for a job.

Hands-On Activity Notes

Activity Online

Complete each step of the inquiry arc below.

Step 1: Developing Questions

After you read each section and analyze the image in the slides, write one question you have about our economy.

My Questions

Section 1: ______________________________

Section 2: ______________________________

Section 3: ______________________________

Section 4: ______________________________

Section 5: ______________________________

Step 2: Planning Your Inquiry

Which of your questions do you want to learn more about? Circle it. Then plan your inquiry below.

People I can ask for help: ______________________________

____

Sources I can use to find information:

1. ______________________________
2. ______________________________
3. ______________________________

Step 3: Gathering and Evaluating Sources

List two trustworthy sources that you found helpful. What information did you learn?

1. ____

____

2. ____

____

Step 4: Making a Claim with Evidence

Write an answer to your question. This is called a claim. Give two pieces of evidence that support your claim.

Claim: ____

____

Evidence from my research:

1. ____

____

2. ____

____

Step 5: Taking Informed Action

Decide how you will communicate your findings to the class or the community. You could make a poster, use presentation software on the computer, or make a video! What other actions might you take?

Summary

You have read about the different parts of a market and that people can buy goods and services. You have learned that a market, such as a farmers' market, is part of a larger economy.

In a market, buyers and sellers come together to get what they want. Buyers have to make choices about what they want to buy. How do you spend your money in a market? What are things that you need and want? How do you choose what to buy?

Show What You Know

Country A

"My name is Kevin. The government in my country tells businesses what to make. It sets prices. There are only a few types of goods and services available. Sometimes, I have to wait in a long line to buy food. The government tells us what types of jobs we can do."

Country B

"My name is Luz. In my country, I decide what type of job I want to do. Businesses choose who they want to hire and how much they want to pay their workers. When I go shopping, there are a wide variety of goods and services from which to choose."

Does Country A or Country B have a free market economy? Write an argument below. Give two pieces of evidence to support your claim.

____

____

____

____

____

____

Lesson 10

Choices in a Free Market

Why do prices change in our economy?

Introduction

Think about the things you have at home. You might have clothes in a dresser. You might even have some toys with which to play. You might have a computer that you can do homework and play games on, or you might have books that you can read. How do you get these things?

People buy things with money. They work so that they can earn money to buy what they need and want. You can also earn money to buy things that you need and want. In a free market economy, people can choose how they earn money.

People can choose what to buy with the money they earn. Sellers also choose what price to charge for the goods or services they provide.

How do sellers decide what prices to charge? Why do some things cost more than others? Why do prices for goods and services sometimes change? In this lesson, you will explore these questions.

Vocabulary

demand
incentive
profit
supply

Sellers can choose the price of these toys. Buyers can purchase these toys with money they earn.

Preview Activity

Activity Online

Think of a good or service that you or your family has purchased recently.

1. Draw the good or service. Label it.

2. How did you or your family earn the money to buy the good or service?

3. What was the benefit to the seller? Why did the seller provide the good or service to you?

4. Did you feel like the price was too high? Too low? About right? Explain why.

Vocabulary Activity

Activity Online

For each term, draw a line to a place in the illustration. Explain how the term relates to that part of the picture. One has been done for you.

demand:

incentive: The buyer could be looking for the best deal. He is motivated to spend less money.

profit:

supply:

Hands-On Activity

Create your own market to discover what happens when supply is high and demand is low. Then find out what happens to prices when supply is low and demand is high.

Directions: The Fruit Market Game (Round 1)

1. **Read Sections 1–2 and then add to your answers in the Preview Activity and Vocabulary Activity.**
2. **With a partner, get ready to play the Fruit Market game.** Half of the pairs will be buyers and half will be sellers. Make sure you have the right Activity Cards!
3. **Play the round.** Sellers want to make as much money as possible. Buyers want to buy as much fruit as possible.
4. **Sing the "Supply and Demand" song.** Learn what happens when supply is high and demand is low.
5. **Read Section 3 and complete your Activity Notes.**

Directions: The Fruit Market Game (Round 2)

1. **Play a second round of the Fruit Market game.**
2. **Sing the "Supply and Demand" song.** Learn what happens when supply is low and demand is high.
3. **Read Section 4 and complete your Activity Notes.** Then read Section 5.

Teachers earn money by providing a service.

1. We Earn Money by Working

Suppose you are at a toy store. You may see a game that you really want to get for you and your friends to play. Like many goods, this game has a price tag that shows how much money you will need to buy it. How can you earn enough money to buy it?

In a free market economy, people choose how to earn their money. The money that people earn is called *income.* Most people earn money by working. They may earn money by providing a service. For example, teachers earn money by teaching students.

At home, you might clean your room every week, help wash dishes, or even take out the garbage. Your parents might pay you an allowance when you complete all of your chores. They are paying you for a service.

People can also earn money by making something and selling it. Think about the things that are in the toy store. You might see action figures, stuffed animals, and toy cars. All of these things are made by people. People then sell these goods to you so that you can use them.

Think about the game that you want to buy. It might cost you $30. You might ask your parents to buy you the game. But your parents have to make money in order to buy things. How do your parents choose to make their money?

Maybe your parents own a business. In a business, people might make or sell goods, or they might help people by offering different services. Businesses pay people for the work that they do. In order to make money to pay people, a business needs to sell something. How do businesses choose what to sell?

This woman earns money by making toys to sell.

2. Businesses and the Economy

Think about the game you want to buy. The business that makes the game earns money when people buy it. But the business also has to spend money to produce the game. The business buys different parts for the game and pays people to put it together.

In a free market economy, businesses want to earn a **profit**. Profit is the amount of money a business has left after it has paid for materials and workers. If a business sells its goods for more than it costs to make them, the business earns a profit.

Often, businesses make choices based on **incentives**. Incentives are things that lead businesses to make certain choices. More profit is one incentive. For example, a business might find a cheaper material with which to make a good. Choosing cheaper materials will increase profits. This is an incentive to make more of this type of good.

Different fabric types and colors can be different prices.

Changes in laws can lead to higher gas prices.

Rules or laws can force a business to spend more money to make its goods. The business might choose to raise prices for the goods it sells. Or, it might choose to make something else instead.

If you want to start your own business to earn money, you must also think about profit. Suppose you want to sell something that will help you earn money for your game. You may choose to open a lemonade stand because lemonade is easy to make. Also, lemonade does not cost very much to make, so you can make a profit.

When you go to the grocery store to get your supplies, you may pick the lemons that cost the least money. Keeping costs low would help you make a profit for each glass of lemonade that you sell. Once you have made your lemonade, for how much do you choose to sell each glass?

To make the most profit, you should choose the lemons that cost less money.

When few people want a good, demand is low.

3. Prices Change When Supply Is High and Demand Is Low

In a free market economy, you can choose the price for which you will sell your lemonade. You could first choose to sell your lemonade for 50¢. If it costs only 5¢ to make each glass, you would make a profit of 45¢ per glass. However, would customers pay 50¢ for a cup of your lemonade?

In a free market, the price for which you choose to sell a good or service is set by both the seller (you) and the buyer (the customer). This is also called **supply** and **demand**. *Supply* is the total amount of a good or service that is available to buy at any price. At your lemonade stand, the supply of lemonade is the amount of lemonade that you make to sell. *Demand* is the total amount of a good or service the customer in the market will buy at all prices.

Together, supply and demand set prices. Think about your new lemonade stand business. You might make five pitchers full of lemonade, so the supply of lemonade is high.

As you sit at your stand, you notice that not many people are buying lemonade from you. In fact, many people might already have lemonade to drink. They might be buying lemonade from a stand nearby, so they do not want to have more lemonade. This makes the demand for lemonade low.

You have a problem now. You have made more lemonade than customers want to buy. What do you think you can do?

One thing that you can do is lower the price of the lemonade. If you make the price of your lemonade low enough, customers might decide to buy some lemonade from you instead of the other stands. You can even make your prices lower than the other lemonade stands to compete with them. Lowering your prices could help you earn money. When supply is high and demand is low, prices go down.

If demand for your lemonade is low, you will need to lower the price of each glass.

Hands-On Activity Notes

Activity Online

Round 1: The Fruit Market Game

Follow these steps to show what happens when **supply is high and demand is low.**

1. Label the buyer and seller in the picture.
2. In the thought bubbles, write what each person is thinking when supply is high and demand is low.
3. Write a new price on the sign to show what happens when supply is high and demand is low.

4. Prices Change When Supply Is Low and Demand Is High

Sometimes, many people want to buy the same thing, but there might not be enough of this good for everyone to buy one. Can you guess what happens to prices when supply is low and demand is high?

Suppose that you have been out at your lemonade stand for a few hours. The day has gotten very hot, and many people have been buying your lemonade. You might have already sold four full pitchers of lemonade, and now you have only one left.

With only one pitcher of lemonade left, your supply of your lemonade is low. But in the hot weather, many customers still want to get lemonade. You might even have a long line of people waiting to buy lemonade from you. The demand for lemonade is high.

When many people want a good, demand is high.

If demand for lemonade is high, you can raise the price of each glass.

Now the customers have a problem. At the price you are charging, kids want more lemonade than you have. The demand for lemonade is greater than the supply that you can sell. That means that not all the customers who are waiting in line will get the lemonade that they want. What do the customers do when supply is low?

Seeing that your supply is low, some customers may be willing to pay more for your lemonade than other customers are. Because some customers are willing to pay more, you might choose to raise the price for your lemonade.

In other words, sellers know that some buyers will pay more for something than other buyers. Because the demand for your lemonade is so high, people will be willing to pay more for it. When demand is high and supply is low, prices go up.

Hands-On Activity Notes

Activity Online

Round 2: The Fruit Market Game

Follow these steps to show what happens when **supply is low and demand is high.**

1. Label the buyer and seller in the picture.
2. In the thought bubbles, write what each person is thinking when supply is low and demand is high.
3. Write a new price on the sign to show what happens when supply is low and demand is high.

5. Changes in Supply and Demand

If the supply of lemons is high, prices will be low.

At your lemonade stand, you learned how supply and demand affect the price for which you sell your lemonade. In a free market economy, supply and demand affect how the prices for all goods and services change.

Suppose that one year California has freezing weather. The cold spoils half of the year's crop of lemons. The supply of lemons is very low. There are not enough lemons for everyone who wants them. The farmers know that customers will pay more to get the lemons they want. So, the farmers decide to raise their prices.

Suppose that the next year farmers in California have grown a huge crop of lemons. There are more lemons than anyone has seen in years. The supply of lemons is very high. The farmers want to sell all their lemons. They know that customers will buy more lemons if the price is lower, so they lower their prices.

Bad weather can change the price of different fruits.

Think about the prices of other things that are affected by supply and demand. The week before Halloween, many people want to buy pumpkins. The demand for pumpkins is higher at this time of year than during any other month. Because demand goes up, prices go up. When Halloween is over, demand goes back down. Then farmers lower their prices so they can sell their pumpkins.

In a free market economy, prices go up and down because of supply and demand. Knowing for what price people can sell their goods and services helps them earn money.

Pumpkins often cost less after Halloween.

Summary

In a free market economy, people can choose how they want to earn money. They can choose to provide a service, or they can choose to make a good. People can also choose to work for a business. Businesses make many choices about how they want to earn money. Incentives and changes in laws can affect the choices that businesses make.

Buyers and sellers, through supply and demand, affect prices in a free market economy. High supply and low demand lead to lower prices. Low supply and high demand lead to higher prices. When either supply or demand changes, prices change, too.

Show What You Know

Explore prices where you live.

1. In the box, draw or paste a picture of a good or service. Write the price.
2. Explain why it has a high or low price. In your answer, use the words *supply* and *demand*.

Price: ______________________

____

____

____

____

____

____

____

____

____

Lesson 11

Using Money Wisely

Why do we save money?

Introduction

Do you do chores at home? If you do, your family may give you an allowance. What would you do with this money you earn?

Some people decide to spend the money they earn right away. They might go to the store and buy a snack or a small toy. But other people choose to save the money that they have earned.

People choose to save money for many reasons. Some people choose to save money in case of an emergency. Others save money because they want to buy something in the future.

Businesses may also choose to save money. Many businesses save money by finding ways to spend less on the goods that they create. They can use the money they save to move to a bigger factory or buy new machines.

People and businesses save money for many reasons. In this lesson, you will explore why and how people and businesses save their money.

Vocabulary

interest

invest

It is important for people to save money. This girl is bringing the money she has saved to the bank.

Preview Activity

Activity Online

Suppose you are walking down the hallway of your school. You look down and see a $5 bill on the floor!

What will you do?

1. Brainstorm at least two options you have.

- ____________________
- ____________________
- ____________________

2. Circle the option you would choose. Then explain why you would make this decision.

Vocabulary Activity

Activity Online

1. Define each term.

interest: ______________________________

____

invest: ______________________________

____

2. Do you think this image better shows interest or investing? Explain.

____

____

____

____

____

____

Hands-On Activity

Analyze a variety of situations dealing with money and create arguments to explain your choice in each situation. Then play a budget game! Allocate tokens to categories and make tough choices.

Directions: Making Economic Choices

1. **In a group of three, read Situation 1 and review the options.**
2. **Complete your Activity Notes.** Make a decision as a group and record your reasoning.
3. **During the class discussion, present your decision and your evidence.**
4. **Take a class vote!** Then discover the consequences of your choice.
5. **Read Section 1.**
6. **Repeat these steps for Situations 2 and 3.**

Directions: Creating a Budget

1. **In a group of three, review a budget plan in your Activity Notes.**
2. **Work together to decide how many tokens to budget for each category.**
3. **Discuss as a class how people make difficult choices while budgeting.**

Hands-On Activity Notes

Activity Online

Situation 1: Birthday Money

It's your birthday! Your grandmother gives you a card. You look inside and see $20. What will you do with the money?

1. With your group, discuss each option. Circle the choice you would make.

   A Use the money to buy something now.

   B Save all the money for later.

   C Spend $10 now. Save $10 for later.

   D Give the money to someone in need.

2. Give two reasons that support your choice.

   • ______________________________

   ____

   • ______________________________

   ____

3. Read Section 1. List two reasons why people save money.

   • ______________________________

   ____

   • ______________________________

   ____

1. People Save Money

If you want to buy a video game system, you will need to save money.

For many people, saving money is not as fun as spending it is. You can choose to spend your money to buy a cookie that you can eat and enjoy right away.

You may also choose to not buy the cookie. Instead, you could choose to put that money aside and save it for later. Why do people choose to save their money rather than spend it?

Many people save so that they can buy something that costs more money than they have at the moment. Suppose you want to buy a new video game system. Video game systems are expensive. In order to buy one, you would need to save some or all of your allowance each week. Saving money allows people to buy things that cost more money.

Another reason that people save money is because they do not know what will happen to them in the future. Suppose you are riding your bike. Suddenly, your bike gets a flat tire. If you have money saved up, you could buy a new tire right away. If not, you will not be able to ride your bike. Saving allows people to pay for things when accidents happen.

Your parents can also save money for you. Some parents or other family members put money aside for when you are old enough to go to college. Doing well in school, even in elementary school, is important. At school, you gain new knowledge and skills. You can use this knowledge and these skills in your life. As you learn more skills at school, you have more opportunities to get better jobs in the future. Saving money for college can help you learn more things later on.

You can use the money that you save to fix your bike.

Activity Online

Situation 2: Saving Your Money

You have started saving the money you receive from gifts and from your allowance. But where should you put it?

1. With your group, discuss each option. Circle the choice you would make.

   A Give the money to your teacher to keep at school.

   B Hide the money at home.

   C Put the money in a bank.

   D Keep the money in a piggy bank in your room.

2. Give two reasons that support your choice.

   - ______________________________
   - ______________________________

3. Read Section 2. List two reasons why it is good to keep your money in a bank.

   - ______________________________
   - ______________________________

2. Ways People Save Money

If you want to save your money, where would you put it? There are many different ways that people choose to save their money.

At home, you can put extra money you have in a jar or a piggy bank. You can use the money you save in the piggy bank to buy something you like in the future.

Piggy banks are a good way to save small amounts of money. Because you can keep a piggy bank at home, you can easily put more money in it. But if you have a piggy bank at home, your money could get lost or even stolen. You may not want to save your money in a piggy bank. Where can you store your money so that it will be safe?

Some people save their money in a piggy bank.

Many people choose to save their money in a bank. A bank is a place where people can store their money safely. If you want to save your money in a bank, your parents can open a savings account for you.

People can save their money in a bank.

Banks offer **interest** on money that you save in your bank account. Suppose you deposit $100 into your savings account at the bank. A year later, you go back to see how much money you have saved. You may be surprised to see that your savings account now has $101. That extra $1 is interest that you earned by saving money at a bank. The more money you store in a bank, the more money you can earn from interest.

The government also protects money in banks. If a bank closes or is robbed, the government will make sure that you do not lose your money.

Activity Online

Situation 3: Investing in Your Business

With the money you saved, you were able to start a business! On weekends, you make and sell lemonade in your neighborhood. What can you do to increase your profits?

1. With your group, discuss each option. Circle the choice you would make.

   A Buy a machine that makes lemonade faster.

   B Raise your prices extremely high.

   C Buy the cheapest lemons you can find.

   D Set aside profits to save up for an emergency.

2. Give two reasons that support your choice.

   - ____
   - ____

3. Read Sections 3 and 4. List two ways that businesses can use their money wisely.

   - ____
   - ____

3. Businesses Use Their Money Wisely

This man is using a machine that helps him make shoes quickly.

Businesses also save money. But where does this extra money come from?

When a business earns a profit, it can choose to put that money back into the business or save some of that profit to use later. Businesses can find ways to spend less on the things they make. They can choose to save this extra money.

One way that a business can spend less money is by using machines. Machines can make goods quickly. By using machines, a business needs less time and money to make a good.

Businesses can also spend less money by choosing different resources to use. A business might find that it can make its goods with cheaper resources. For example, a business could make shirts from cotton instead of linen since cotton is cheaper.

Cotton is a natural resource that a business can use to make clothing.

4. Businesses Invest Their Money

Spending less money helps businesses of all sizes do well. What can a business do with the money that it sets aside?

A business can **invest** the money it sets aside. When a business invests its money back into the business, it tries to make even more money.

One way to make even more money is to buy new machines so that goods are made faster. For example, the owner of a business may already own a machine. But the owner may find that a new machine would help her make twice as many goods as she can now. If she has saved enough money, the owner can invest by buying a new machine. This machine will help the business make more money in the future.

Machines break down sometimes, and a business needs to pay someone to fix them. If the business has saved its money, it can fix a broken machine. When the machine is repaired, the business can continue to make goods to sell.

This man is a fixing a broken elevator so that people can use it.

Companies invent new things to make computers better and faster.

Businesses save their money so that they can invest in creating new things to sell. In a free market economy, businesses compete with one another by inventing new and useful goods or services.

Do you have a computer at home? Many different businesses make computers and compete with one another to get people to buy their goods. They often spend money each year to invent new ways to make their computers better and faster.

If businesses save, they can spend that money to invent new ways to make their goods better. Businesses save money so that they can make better goods to sell to their customers.

Hands-On Activity Notes

Activity Online

Work in a group of three. Follow the directions on the slide to make and revise a budget.

Savings

1 token	2 tokens	3 tokens
Save a small amount.	Save a medium amount.	Save a large amount.

My Budget

Entertainment

1 token	2 tokens	3 tokens
Buy cheap phone apps.	Buy board games.	Buy video games.

My Budget

Food

1 token	2 tokens	3 tokens
Eat at fast food restaurants.	Cook at home.	Eat at sit-down restaurants.

My Budget

Clothing

1 token	2 tokens	3 tokens
Mend your current clothes.	Buy clothes at a discount store.	Buy clothes at a department store.

My Budget

School Supplies

1 token	2 tokens	3 tokens
Use supplies from last year.	Buy supplies at a discount store.	Buy supplies at an office store.

My Budget

Donations to Charity

1 token	2 tokens	3 tokens
Donate a small amount of money.	Donate a medium amount of money.	Donate a large amount of money.

My Budget

Summary

Many people choose to save their money instead of spending it. People save their money so that they can buy something expensive in the future, or they put money aside in case they need to fix something that breaks. They can save this money in a bank.

Businesses save money by finding ways to spend less on making goods. They can choose to use machines or choose cheaper resources. Then they can save this money for new machines or to invent new things.

Show What You Know

Draw a picture of something you would like to invest in for your future. Then, write about how you plan to do it.

Lesson 12

The United States and Global Trade

How does global trade affect our economy?

Introduction

How many countries does it take to get you to school in the morning? The alarm you use to wake up may be from South Korea. You may get dressed in jeans and a T-shirt that were made in China. When you put on your shoes, they may have been made in Thailand.

As part of your breakfast, you could eat a banana that was grown in Ecuador. The orange juice that you drink may be from oranges grown in another part of the United States. When you get a ride to school, it may be in a car designed in Germany. The gas in the car may come from oil found in Canada.

By the time you arrive at school, you probably have used things that came from many different countries. In this lesson, you will learn how these things get to your community.

Vocabulary

global trade
manufactured

The different foods you eat can be from places all around the world.

Preview Activity

Activity Online

Look at the map below. At the head of each arrow, draw a picture of a product that comes from the country the arrow represents. Use the text in the Introduction or conduct your own research.

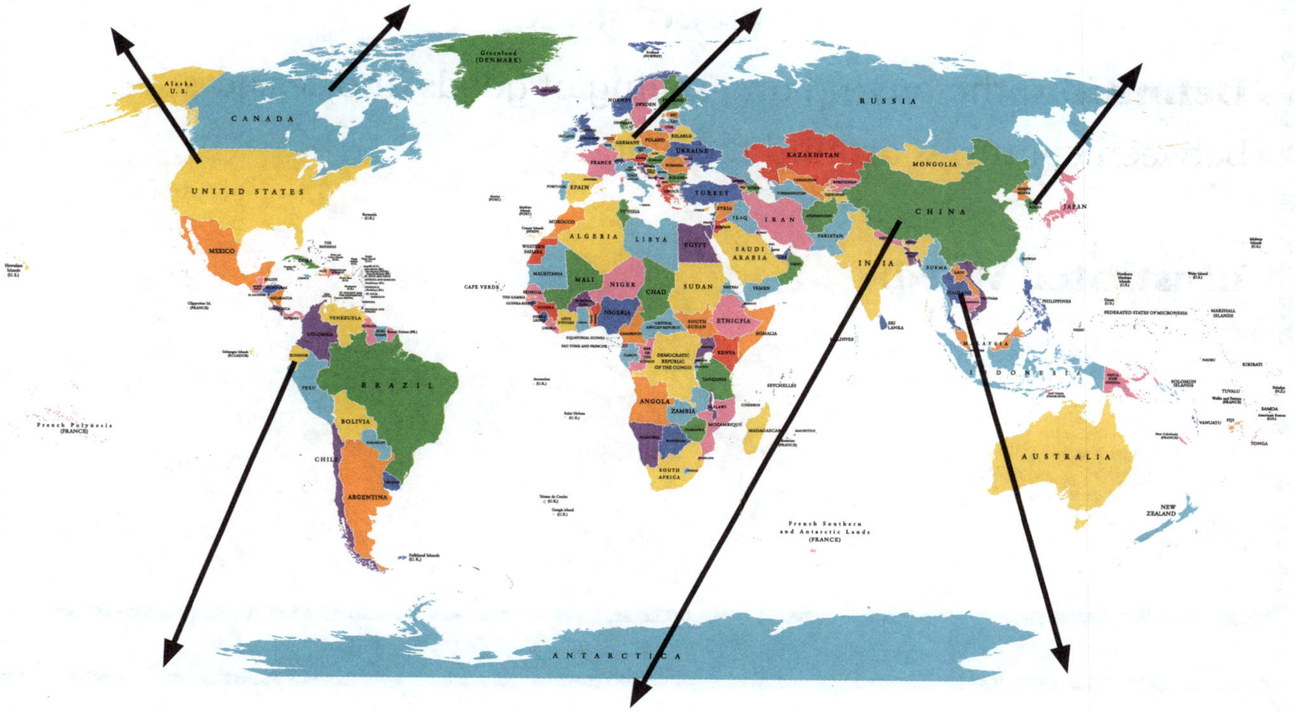

List three other items you would like to know more about.

1. ______________________________

2. ______________________________

3. ______________________________

Vocabulary Activity

Activity Online

Create an "illustrated word" that shows the meaning of each term.

For example, to show the term *increase,* you might write the word with each letter getting larger. Example: increase

global trade

Definition: the buying and selling of goods and services between countries around the world

Illustrated Word:

manufactured

Definition: made with machines

Illustrated Word:

Hands-On Activity

Use a ball of yarn to create a trade web connecting countries around the world to one another. Identify different points of view about trade, and then write an argument analyzing global trade.

Directions: Global Trading Game

1. **Set up the game.** Sit in a circle. Each student represents a different country and gets trading cards showing what his or her country produces.
2. **Learn the rules and play a trading game.** Follow the directions on the slide.
3. **Discuss the game and make connections to the real world.**
4. **Read Sections 1–3.** Learn why countries trade and what they trade.

Directions: Perspectives on Trade

1. **With a partner, read Sections 4–5.** Learn pros and cons of trade.
2. **In your Activity Notes, compare two points of view about global trade.** Then draw the faces and describe each point of view.
3. **Research to find out more about global trade.** What seems fair or unfair?
4. **Write an argument explaining whether you think global trade is good or bad.** Make sure to give evidence to support your position.
5. **Share your argument with the class.** Listen to other students' arguments.

1. Countries Trade What They Have for What They Want

Have you ever traded things with your friends? Maybe you traded an apple for a banana at lunch. Or maybe you traded a toy for a game. Why did you trade with your friend?

When people trade with one another, they give things they have to get things they want. Different countries can trade with each other, too. For example, Ecuador is a country that trades with the United States. Ecuador grows a lot of bananas. The United States does not grow bananas, but people in the United States want to eat this fruit. So, the United States buys bananas from Ecuador.

What does Ecuador want? Farmers in Ecuador need tractors. The United States has many factories that make tractors. So, Ecuador buys tractors from the United States.

Bananas from Ecuador can be traded for tractors from the United States.

Many goods travel on container ships like this one.

Ecuador sells bananas to the United States. The United States sells tractors to Ecuador. You could say that Ecuador trades its bananas for tractors. In the same way, the United States trades its tractors for bananas.

These kinds of trades go on all around the world. Countries have traded with one another for hundreds of years. This is called **global trade**. Today, global trade is bigger than ever before. One reason for this is that people have figured out better ways to move and store goods.

As global trade grows, countries around the world rely on each other more and more. The United States wants bananas, and Ecuador has more bananas than it wants. Ecuador wants tractors, and the United States has more tractors than it wants. The United States and Ecuador can now trade with one another, and both countries are better off as a result.

Oil drills help dig up oil for people to use.

2. Countries Trade Natural Resources

Countries have different natural resources. They trade resources that they have for ones that they need or want.

Bananas are an example of a natural resource that can be found in Ecuador. They grow best in hot and wet countries, like Ecuador. That is why Ecuador has many bananas to sell. The United States buys most of its bananas from countries like Ecuador.

Oil, gold, and copper are also resources. The United States has a large supply of oil, gold, and copper, but people still want to have more. So, the United States buys these resources from other countries. For example, Saudi Arabia has a lot of oil. South Africa has many gold and diamond mines. Chile sells more copper than any other country in the world. The United States buys resources from all these countries. In return, it sells to these countries things that they want to buy.

The United States has its own resources to sell. For example, wheat grows very well in parts of the United States. The United States can grow and sell a lot of wheat to other countries.

Sometimes, natural resources can be found only at certain times of the year. Grapes need warm weather to grow. During the summer, the United States produces many grapes. It does not need to buy grapes from other places. The United States even sells some of its summer grapes to other countries. But during the winter, the United States has to buy grapes from warmer countries, such as Chile and Mexico. Global trade lets people in the United States enjoy grapes all year.

Many grapes in the United States, such as these, come from Chile.

This car is sold in the United States, but it was designed in Germany.

3. Countries Trade Goods That They Make

In addition to natural resources, countries also trade goods that they make. Some of these goods are made by hand. People make jewelry, clothing, and art that they can trade with people in other countries.

Countries can also trade **manufactured** goods, or goods made in factories. Cars, watches, and shoes are all made in factories. Can you think of other examples?

Why do countries trade for goods that are made somewhere else? One reason is that some countries are known for their high-quality goods. Switzerland is famous for its fine watches. Many people like to buy phones made in South Korea. Germany and the United States design many different types of cars. Some companies in the United States are also known for making very good computers.

A country may also trade for goods that are made someplace else so that it can save money. Some countries can make goods for less money than other countries can. For example, many Chinese businesses make clothes at a low cost. These businesses often pay their workers less money than businesses in the United States do. These businesses can also purchase materials at a cheaper price. Cheaper labor and materials lower the price of clothes made in China.

Countries may also buy goods from other countries because they are priced low. This is one reason your jeans, T-shirts, and sneakers may come from countries in Asia.

These people are making clothes in a factory in Asia.

4. Business and Global Trade

Global trade has given companies the opportunity to begin selling their goods in places around the world. Businesses have also changed the way they make and sell goods.

You might choose to buy clothes made by an American company. But when you check your clothing's tag, you may find that it was actually made in a country on the other side of the world. Why does this American company make your clothes in another country?

Some American companies find that they can make more profit by building factories in other countries. In some countries, materials are cheaper and workers are not paid as much as they are in the United States. Because production costs are lower, businesses save money when making goods.

Labels like these tell us where the things we buy are made.

Starbucks is an American company, but they opened many stores around the world, such as this one in India.

Many times, businesses open stores in other countries so that they can sell their goods to more people. For example, there are many businesses that started in the United States. If these businesses want to sell goods to people in other countries, they may open stores in other countries.

One reason companies can be found around the world is because of changes in the way people communicate. In the past, company owners could not easily talk to their workers if a factory was far away from them. Today, phones and computers allow people to easily talk around the world. Companies in the United States can easily tell people in a factory in another country what to do. Because of this, many businesses have shops and factories in many different countries.

5. Benefits and Costs of Global Trade

There are many benefits for countries that trade with each other. Global trade allows people to buy things from all over the world. It allows people to buy quality goods and goods that are low-cost. Without global trade, we would not be able to have bananas for breakfast all year long, and the prices of the things we want, such as clothes, shoes, and cars, would go up.

But global trade has many costs as well. It allows companies to move factories to countries where they can pay their workers less money. Moving factories to other countries can take jobs away from workers in home countries. It can also keep pay low for workers in other countries.

These workers are making cars in Germany.

Suppose a shoe company in the United States moves its factories to Thailand. What happens? The company saves money and new jobs become available for the people of Thailand. But American workers who make shoes may lose their jobs.

Also, global trade means that people do not always buy things that are made locally. When shopping for fruit, people often choose to buy bananas from Ecuador. But even though there are costs to global trade, it brings together the people and countries of the world.

These people are fighting for American workers who might lose their jobs when companies move factories to other countries.

Hands-On Activity Notes

Activity Online

Show each person's point of view about global trade.

- Draw each face to show how the person feels.
- In the thought bubble, write what the person is thinking.

Person in the United States who buys a watch made in Switzerland

Person in Vietnam who works in a shoe factory

Is global trade good or bad? Write an argument. Give evidence to support your position.

Summary

Global trade connects countries around the world. Countries trade what they have for what they want. They trade natural resources and goods they make. Businesses can also sell different goods or build factories in countries around the world.

Global trade allows people to buy quality and low-cost goods from other places, but some countries may lose businesses and jobs to other countries. In some countries, global trade may keep workers' pay low. However, all countries are often better off because of global trade.

Show What You Know

Look at the labels on products in your house, school, or a store. Find two products that came from another part of the world. Then follow these steps:

1. Complete these sentences with the names of two products and the countries those products came from.

   We get ________________ from the country of ________________.

   We get ________________ from the country of ________________.

2. Find the two countries on the world map. Color in the countries.
3. Draw a sketch of your first item. Put the sketch near the country on the map where the item came from. Do the same thing for your second item.
4. Draw a dot on the map to show where your community is located. Draw an arrow from each sketch to your community.
5. Give your map a title.

Flip the page →

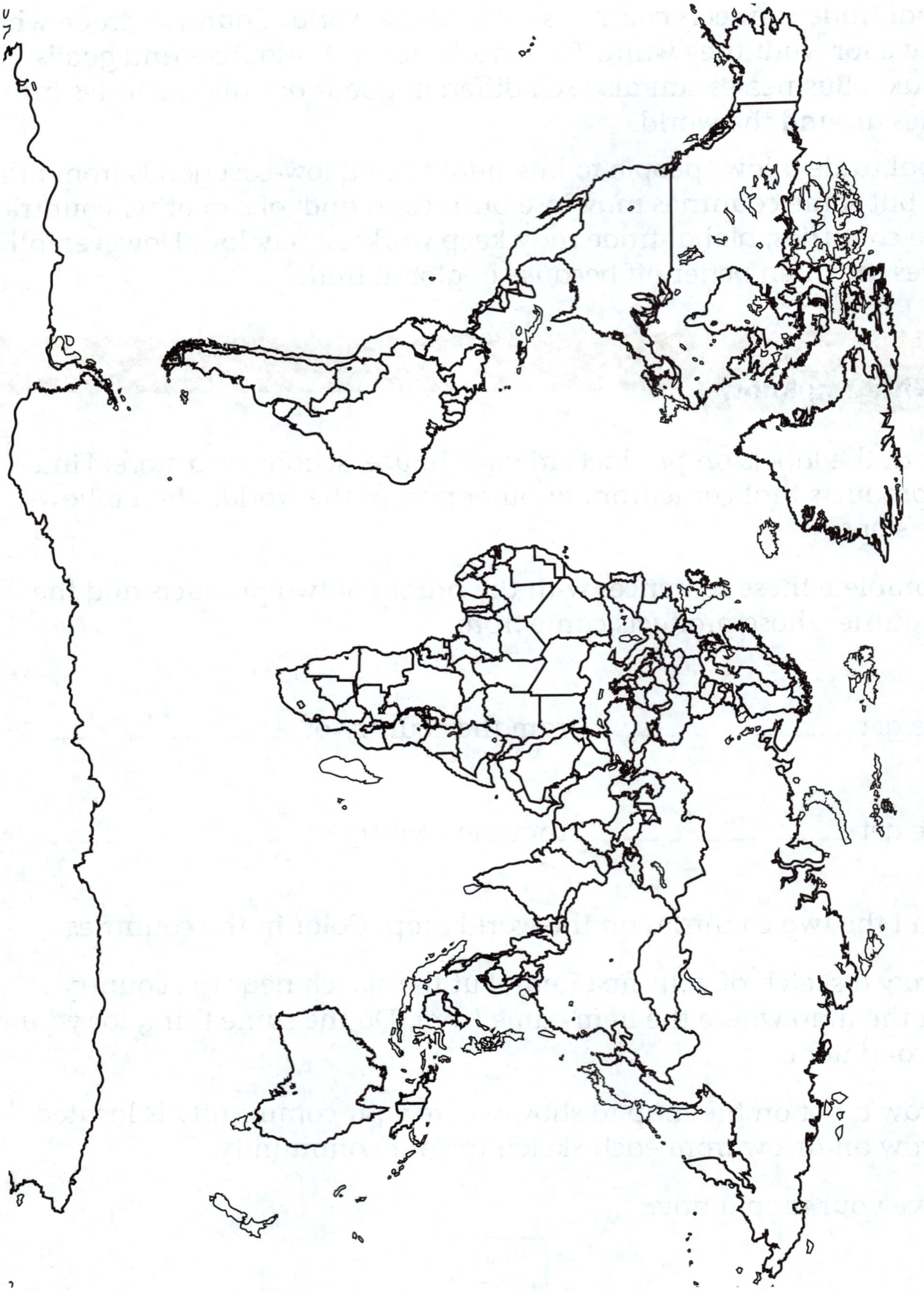

Title: ______________________

Unit 4

Civics

Explore different community services and rank their importance. Plan and write a podcast about government. Bring to life important steps in being a good citizen, such as speaking at a public meeting. Plan and carry out a service project to make a difference in the world. Conduct an inquiry to find out why it is important to be a good citizen.

Unit Inquiry Project

1 Gathering Visual Evidence

What do you see in this image?	
What do these people appear to be doing?	
Why might they collect food and clothing?	

2 Developing the Compelling Question

Unit Storyline

Close to 11 million children in the United States do not get enough food each day. Many of the families who suffer get help from programs at the federal, state, and local level. What role can leaders play in addressing hunger? What role can voters play? What role can you play?

Unit Compelling Question

How can being an active citizen benefit others?

List three questions you have about the Unit Storyline and Compelling Question.

1.

2.

3.

3 Collecting Evidence

After you complete each lesson, return to this table and answer the questions. You will be gathering key information that will help you complete the Unit Inquiry Project.

Lesson	Supporting Questions	What I Learned
13 Providing Public Services	What are some types of public services and how are they paid for? How do public services support people in your community?	
14 Government in the United States	How can you take an active role in government at a local level? State level? National level?	
15 Citizenship and Participation	Why is it important to be an informed voter who picks good leaders? What are other ways that you can be a good citizen?	
16 Making a Difference in the World	What are little things you can do everyday that make a difference? How can you help solve big challenges in your community and the world?	

4 Building Additional Content Knowledge

Gather and evaluate additional sources to answer the Unit Compelling Question: *How can being an active citizen benefit others?*

You may conduct outside research or use these readings from *Social Studies Alive! Our Community and Beyond* Social Studies Stories:

- Eagles, Flags, and Midnight Parades
- Helping a Community in Need
- The Constitution Protects Our Rights
- Making Your Voice Count

Source Title(s)	
Additional Evidence	

5 Constructing an Argument

Write a sentence answering the Unit Compelling Question: *How can being an active citizen benefit others?* This is called a claim.

Then provide at least two pieces of evidence to support your claim. Your evidence can come from the activities you did in class, the readings you completed in your Student Journal or Social Studies Stories, or additional research that you conducted.

Claim:

Evidence:

6 Taking Informed Action

Decide how you want to share what you learned. You could make a poster, a digital presentation, or a video. You might share your presentation with your classmates or with adults in the community.

Lesson 13

Providing Public Services

What different services does our community have?

Introduction

You can find services in your community. Services are tasks that other people do for you. Some businesses sell services to people. They may offer plumbing and cleaning services. Even chefs in restaurants provide a service. You have to pay to use these services.

Other services are offered to everyone. These are usually provided by a government. Cities, states, and the United States all have their own governments that provide services.

People can use the services a government provides for free or at a low cost. This is because every person in a community helps to pay for these services.

What are some of the services that governments offer? And how do we pay for them? You'll find out in this lesson.

Vocabulary

- **first responder**
- **private service**
- **public service**
- **suburb**
- **tax**

Millions of American children are educated in public schools every year. Education is an example of a public service in the United States.

Preview Activity

Activity Online

Write the service that each photo represents in a typical community.

1. ____________________

2. ____________________

3. ____________________

4. ____________________

5. ____________________

6. ____________________

Vocabulary Activity

Activity Online

Complete the news article with the correct terms.

Vocabulary Word Bank

first responders | private services | public services
suburbs | tax

THE COMMUNITY ORACLE

Volume 27 Issue 49

Firefighters Save Walnut Grove Elementary

A fire at Walnut Grove Elementary was put out by Fire Station #3 last week. The damage was not terrible. The teacher lounge had some smoke damage, and the cafeteria had some light damage, too.

Principal Skinner was quoted as saying, "We are lucky to have ______________________ in our community to save us in emergency situations."

Fire Station #3 recently received funds to buy a new fire engine, thanks to the income ______________________ that residents pay.

Mayor Alejandra Lopez congratulated the firefighters while saying, "It's not just big cities that need these heroes. A community like ours in the ______________________ does, too."

Of course, firefighters are just one of a handful of

____

that support every person. Our community also has many ______________________ , or businesses, like the grocery store. We are lucky to live in such a fine community.

Hands-On Activity

Explore why people join communities and how public services are paid for. Learn about six different public services and rank their importance.

Directions: Communities and Taxes

1. **Fly over a town to take a quick glance at its community.**
2. **Read Section 1.** Learn about why people join communities.
3. **Complete your Activity Notes.** Provide four reasons that people join communities.
4. **Fly over the town again to look for private and public services.**
5. **Read Section 2.** Learn about taxes and why they are important.

Directions: Public Services and Their Importance

1. **Study an Activity Card with your partner.** Examine each image.
2. **Connect it to a public service.** Which public service is related to all of the images?
3. **Read the section that corresponds to your public service.** Learn more about the public service.
4. **Complete your Activity Notes for that section.** Find the row that matches your Activity Card and fill in all of the information.
5. **Repeat Steps 1–5 until you have completed all six public services.**

1. Why We Form Communities

Neighbors help people feel accepted.

Why do people choose to live together? There are many benefits that come with living in a community.

Living in a community provides people with security. Police and firefighters make sure that citizens are always safe.

In communities, there are different rules and laws. Laws promote safety and make sure that people have the rights they deserve. Citizens come together to make laws.

Communities give people a feeling of acceptance. It feels good to know that there are people who care about you. People in communities become friends with their neighbors and coworkers.

Neighbors look out for each other. If people have problems, they can go to a neighbor for help.

People can usually find jobs in their community. People need jobs so that they can make a living. They work to make money, which they need to purchase important goods and services.

Communities also give people easy access to services. Individuals can provide **private services** for a community. Getting a haircut at a barber shop is an example of a private service. But a community's government also has **public services** for everyone living there. Some examples of public services are providing clean water and electricity.

This librarian is making a living and helping his community at the same time.

Hands-On Activity Notes

Activity Online

In a postcard to a friend, provide four reasons that people join communities.

Dear ______________________________,

I learned all about communities and why people join them.

Here are four reasons:

1. ______________________________

2. ______________________________

3. ______________________________

4. ______________________________

2. Paying for Public Services

Governments provide public services to communities. However, it costs money to provide these services. How do governments pay for public services?

Public services are paid for with **taxes**. Taxes are money that people and businesses pay to a government. Cities, states, and the United States all have governments. They each collect their own taxes.

There are many different kinds of taxes. One important kind of tax is income tax. This tax is based on how much money someone makes. People who make more money pay more income tax.

This man is paying his income tax with the help of a computer and phone.

This family is looking to buy new clothes. They will need to pay sales tax in addition to the price of the clothes.

Another type of tax is sales tax. Sales tax is a fee that is added when people purchase goods and services. For example, when you buy new clothes, you must also pay a sales tax.

Property taxes are paid by people who own land. All homeowners have to pay property taxes. People who rent their apartment or home do not need to pay a property tax.

Taxes pay for the public services that communities use every day. Communities and their leaders come together to discuss taxes. They talk about what goods and services they want to be public services. Next, you will learn some of the public services that are available in many communities.

This police officer has stopped a driver for not following the rules of the road.

3. Police

All communities need to keep the peace. Police provide this service.

Police keep the peace in several ways. They make sure that people obey laws. For example, police give tickets to drivers who don't stop at red lights. Police walk or ride through neighborhoods to make sure people are safe. They arrest people who steal or commit other crimes.

Police also help people in other ways. They direct traffic and give directions to people who are lost. They help rescue people when floods, earthquakes, and other disasters happen.

Police around the United States are alike in many ways. However, they are also different. Some police ride in police cars. Others ride motorcycles, bicycles, and even horses. Some police officers patrol the highways, while others focus on protecting people and their neighborhoods.

Many police officers are heroes in their communities. In 2012, one officer from West Covina, California, saved a choking baby before catching a bank robbery suspect 30 minutes later! The officer got a 911 call saying a young child was having trouble breathing. He saved the baby before catching up to the suspect in a car chase. The officer was awarded a medal from the police department for his actions.

These police officers both work in New York City, but they get around very differently. One rides a horse, while the other uses a motorcycle.

4. Health Care

In the United States, people can get some kinds of health care as a public service. Taxes help to pay for health care for older people and people with lower incomes. Veterans, or former members of the military, and children can have some of their care provided by public services.

There are public hospitals where people can get care for free or at a low cost. Towns and cities may offer other services, such as free flu shots. If people need emergency care, they can get help at a hospital even if they can't pay for it.

This elderly woman is receiving care from her doctor. Older people can receive some types of care as a public service.

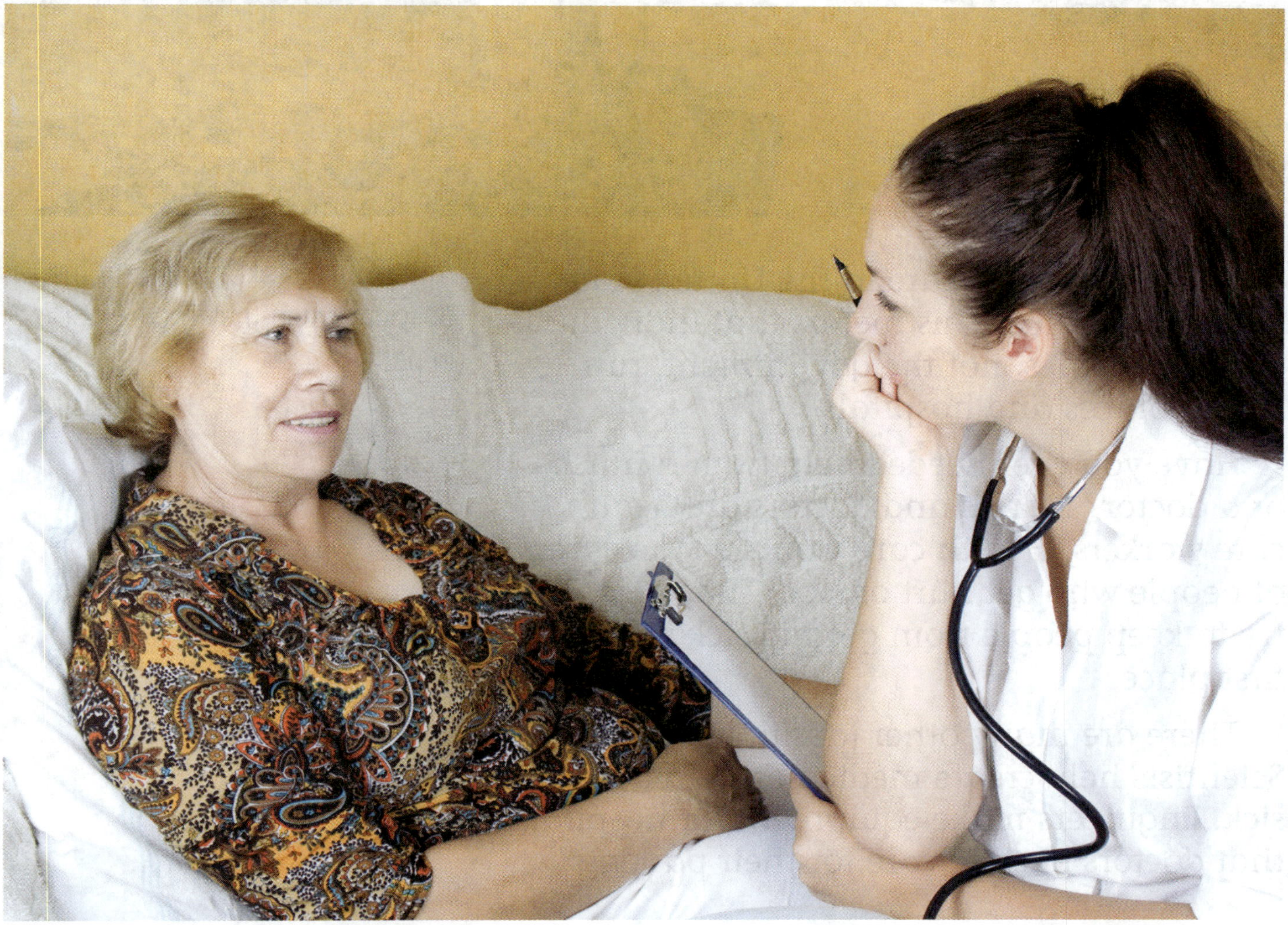

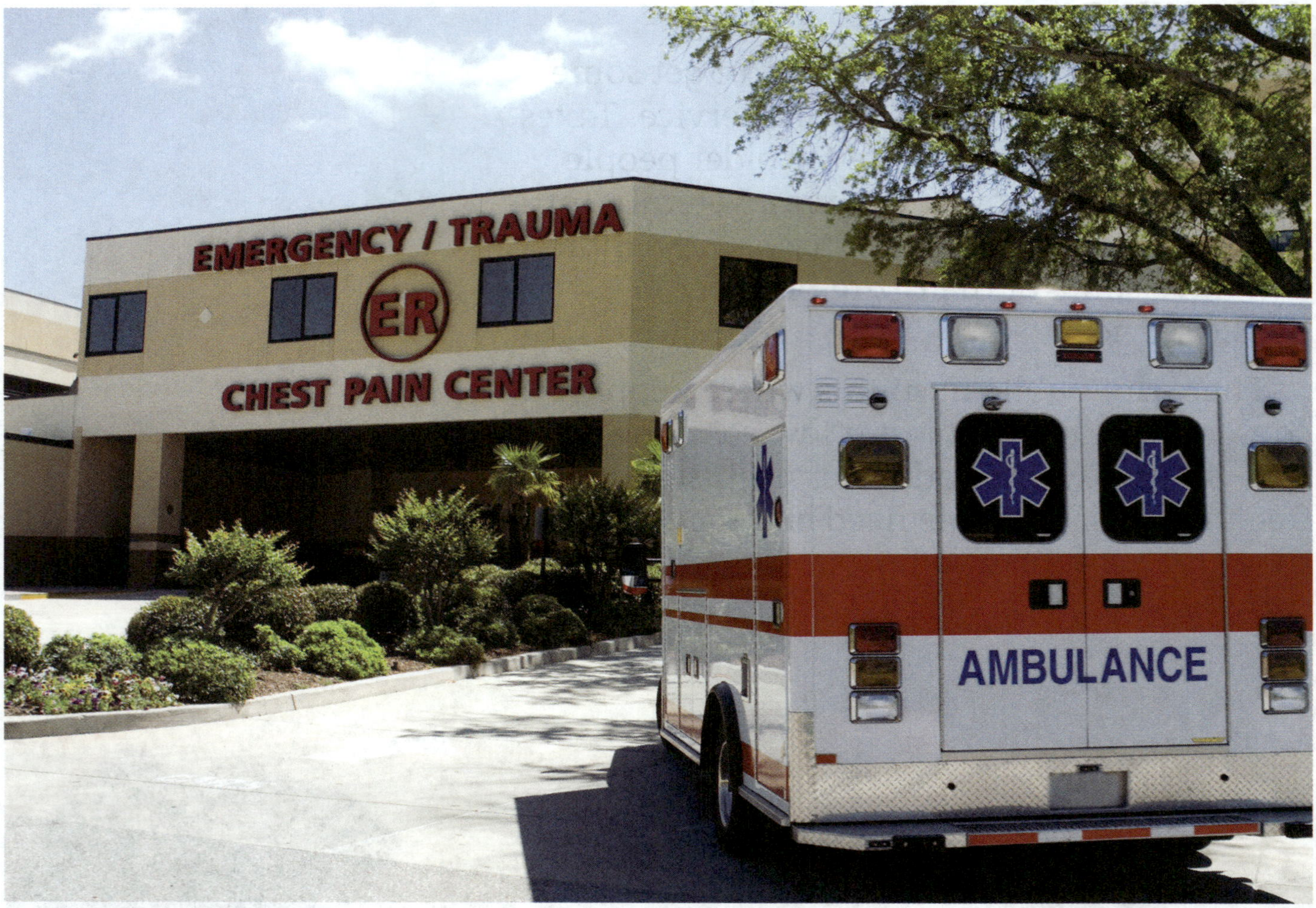

Ambulances take people to the hospital when they are sick or in pain.

But most health care in the United States is a private service. This means that individuals and companies, not the government, run doctor offices and hospitals.

Have you ever needed help from a nurse or a doctor? Nurses and doctors are health care workers. Health care workers take care of people who get hurt or sick. They also try to keep people from getting sick in the first place.

There are many other jobs in health care. Scientists help create medicines to treat the sick. Engineers make equipment for hospitals that doctors need to care for their patients.

5. Public Schools

In kindergarten, children begin to learn how to read and write. Students in public school use a public service.

Do you go to a public school? If so, then you are getting a public service.

Money from taxes pays for public schools. The whole community pays these taxes, not just the families of students.

Public schools do a very important job for the community. Schools teach students many useful skills, such as how to read, write, and do math. Students will need these skills to get good jobs and to be helpful members of the community.

In the United States, you can go to public schools from kindergarten through high school. After high school, you might choose to go to a public college. You would have to pay part of the cost, and taxes would help pay the rest.

You can also go to a private school or college. These schools don't get money from taxes. Instead, they charge students and their families for their services.

Until about 1850, most schools in the United States were private schools. If students didn't have enough money, they didn't go to school. In most places, only boys went to school.

Many things have changed since then. Today, people agree that everyone needs a good education. This agreement is why the government provides schools as a public service.

These students are graduating from high school. They might attend either a public or private college.

6. Firefighting

Firefighting is an important service. Putting out fires takes a lot of skills, training, and courage. Firefighters around the world often risk their lives to do their job.

Many places still use volunteers to fight fires. But towns and cities may hire trained firefighters as a public service. They also buy equipment for fighting fires.

Firefighters try to keep fires from starting in the first place. They teach people what to do to prevent fires and to make sure that people obey fire safety laws.

Firefighters risk their lives on a daily basis to keep our communities safe.

New York City firefighters were first responders to the events of September 11th.

Firefighters help communities in other ways, too. They help take care of people who are hurt in accidents. They also help people after disasters such as floods and earthquakes.

On September 11, 2001, terrorists crashed two planes into the World Trade Center in New York City. The New York Fire Department, which is a public service, sent firefighters to the World Trade Center. These firefighters were **first responders**. Many of them lost their lives trying to save people from the wreckage. Their acts of courage are still remembered today.

The San Francisco cable cars are a form of public transportation. They have been running for more than 100 years.

7. Public Transportation

People need to get from place to place in towns and cities across the United States. Governments often try to help by offering public transportation.

Many cities have public buses. Some cities also have streetcars, which are small trains that use city streets. Larger cities often have subways. Subways are trains that run under the ground. Some places have trains and buses that run between cities and the **suburbs**. Suburbs are communities that form on the edges of cities.

In most places, you must pay to use public transportation. But the cost is usually low so that most people can afford it.

Public transportation helps people get around without using cars. Most car engines make the air dirty. When there are fewer cars on the street, the air is cleaner.

Many cities are making it easier for people to use bicycles instead of driving cars. In some cities, you can even rent a bicycle for a low cost. Some people ride bikes to get to public buses and trains. Then they park and lock the bikes, or even bring them along for the ride.

This man is using both his bicycle and public transportation to get around.

8. Public Parks

Have you ever played in a public park? If you have, then you have used a popular public service.

Why do governments spend tax money on parks? Parks bring us many benefits. They add beauty and a touch of nature to our cities and towns. Parks also give us space for all kinds of activities.

Public parks provide a place for people to run and play.

Imagine spending a sunny Saturday afternoon in a large city park. You see families having picnics and people walking their dogs. Skaters scoot along the park's paths. You see a softball game and a soccer match. You pass a band playing on an outdoor stage while people dance. In a playground area, parents talk while their children play on the swings and slides. On a pretty lake, people are rowing boats. Where else in a city can people do so many fun and healthy things?

Community gardens provide neighbors a place to work together.

Parks are useful for another reason. They bring people together and help create good feelings in a community. Some parks even have community gardens. There, neighbors can work side by side growing flowers, herbs, fruits, and vegetables.

Hands-On Activity Notes

Complete each row as you examine each Activity Card.

Images	**Public Service**	**My Ranking (circle one)**
		1. very important 2. somewhat important 3. not very important
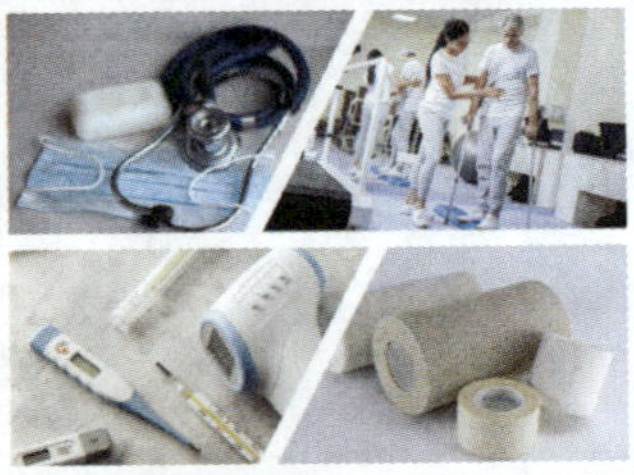		1. very important 2. somewhat important 3. not very important
		1. very important 2. somewhat important 3. not very important
		1. very important 2. somewhat important 3. not very important
		1. very important 2. somewhat important 3. not very important
		1. very important 2. somewhat important 3. not very important

Activity Online

Evidence for My Ranking
1. **2.**
1. **2.**
1. **2.**
1. **2.**
1. **2.**
1. **2.**

Summary

There are many reasons why people live in communities. One of them is that communities offer public services. Governments raise money for these services by collecting taxes. Cities, states, and the United States all have their own taxes.

Police and firefighters keep people safe. Health care services help people who are sick or hurt. Public schools teach students skills they need to get good jobs in the future. Public transportation helps people get from place to place without using cars. Parks give people places to play and to enjoy nature. What are the public services where you live?

Show What You Know

Choose a public service in your community. In the space below, make a poster that shows how this service helps your community. Include these things on your poster:

- ❑ the name of the public service
- ❑ a description of how the service helps the community
- ❑ a picture that illustrates the service

Lesson 14

Government in the United States

How is our government set up?

Introduction

Does your community have a park? Have you played or taken a walk there? The park may be provided by your local government.

Your local government helps run your community. It helps keep people safe and provides services. It helps build roads and public schools. If you have an idea to improve your community, you can bring the idea to your mayor or city council.

What if you have an idea to improve your state? What if you have an idea to help your country? Your state has its own government, too. So does the country. The country's government is known as the federal government. In this lesson, you'll learn about how the government is set up in your community, your state, and our country.

Vocabulary

- **city hall**
- **Constitution**
- **federal government**
- **legislature**
- **local government**
- **public works**
- **state government**
- **tribal government**

City leaders help run New York City's local government.

Preview Activity

Activity Online

After listening to the podcast, answer these questions about Peter and his involvement with the park.

PODCAST
Episode 221

In this episode, our guest, Peter, talks about his plans to get the city to build a new playground in the park that he could use.

Whose support in the city government will Peter need to get?

____

____

Who do you think Peter would go to if the park was a state park?

____

____

Who do you think Peter would go to if the park was a national park?

____

____

Vocabulary Activity

Activity Online

Complete each podcast description with the correct term.

Vocabulary Word Bank

city hall · Constitution · federal government · legislature · local government · public works · state government · tribal government

EPISODE 1: Who Picks Our State Bird?

Did you know that the state ______________ is responsible for picking our state motto, flag, and bird because they write laws? In this episode, we'll be spending time with people from the ______________.

EPISODE 2: Takin' It to the Streets

In this episode, we will explore the freedom of speech, press, assembly, and religion. We will have congressional leaders from the ______________ on the show. They will be telling us about our many rights in the Bill of Rights, which is part of the ______________.

EPISODE 3: Debating a Pool or Playground

This is a special podcast taken from ______________, where the city council was meeting. Listen as they debate a new ______________ project. Should it be a pool or a playground? Our special guest, Peter Seong, has his opinion! He will share with us what he and the members of the ______________ talked about.

EPISODE 4: Meeting with the Council

We're going to visit a local reservation and speak with members of the ______________. They will tell us all about how the tribal council has created police and fire departments.

Hands-On Activity

Activity Online

Plan and write a podcast about government.

Directions: Creating a Podcast About Our Government

1. **Read Sections 1–4.** Learn about the different levels of government.
2. **In pairs, discuss the different services provided at the different levels of government.** What service does each level of government offer?
3. **Complete your Activity Notes.** Plan a podcast to teach others about one level of government and what it does. Make sure to complete each step:
    - Set up your podcast
    - Plan what to ask
    - Plan what to say

City halls are where local governments have their offices.

1. Local Government

Does your community have a **city hall**? Maybe it's called a town hall where you live. This building is where your community's government has its offices. There, you'll find the people who keep your city or town running smoothly.

Your city's or town's government is an example of **local government**. This is the government made up of people who live and work in your community. Another type of local government is county government. A county is larger than a city. It is made up of nearby cities, towns, or rural areas.

Local government provides you and your neighbors with many services. It runs your library, keeps local parks looking nice, and supports police and firefighters. It provides trash removal, sewage treatment, and water for you to drink. It also builds and repairs local roads. Your local government does many of the jobs you depend on each day.

Your local government tries to make your community a safe and fun place to live. Its most important job is to make laws. Laws tell people what they can do and cannot do. For example, one law may say people must clean up after their pets. Another law may say how fast people can drive near a school.

The community library is a service provided by local governments.

People vote for leaders to run the government. They may vote for a mayor or city council to lead their city. A school board may be elected to make decisions for schools. A sheriff may be elected to support law enforcement.

Many other workers help the government run. The police help make sure that people obey the law. Firefighters help keep people safe. People in other departments have their own special work to do.

All these people need money to do their jobs. The money comes from taxes. The mayor and the city council know how much money there is to spend. They decide how much money to give to each part of the city's government.

2. State Government

Your local government has many parts to keep your community running smoothly. Your state also needs to run smoothly, which is why each state in the United States has its own government.

Each state has a state constitution. This document sets up the **state government**. It describes each part of the state's government.

In each state, people elect a governor to help lead the state. The governor proposes the state budget, appoints officials, and carries out laws.

The governor works with the state's **legislature** to run the state. The legislature is the part of the government that makes laws. People from communities around the state vote for leaders to be part of the state's legislature.

Your state also has a court system to make decisions about what a law means. Courts make sure that laws affect everyone in the state fairly. Judges may be elected or appointed to a court.

The people elect the governor of the state. Here, Governor Laura Kelly of Kansas gives a speech.

State governments maintain state parks like the Ichetucknee Springs State Park in Florida.

Local governments provide public services to a city or town, but state governments provide services for everyone in the state. People pay taxes to the state to fund these services.

States have an education department. Each state helps provide schools to teach students. States also have colleges and universities.

Like local governments, states have a department to maintain **public works**. The department builds roads that cross the entire state to connect cities and towns. It also finds ways to get water to everyone in the state.

States provide many other services, too. Each state has a highway patrol, issues driver licenses, and takes care of state parks.

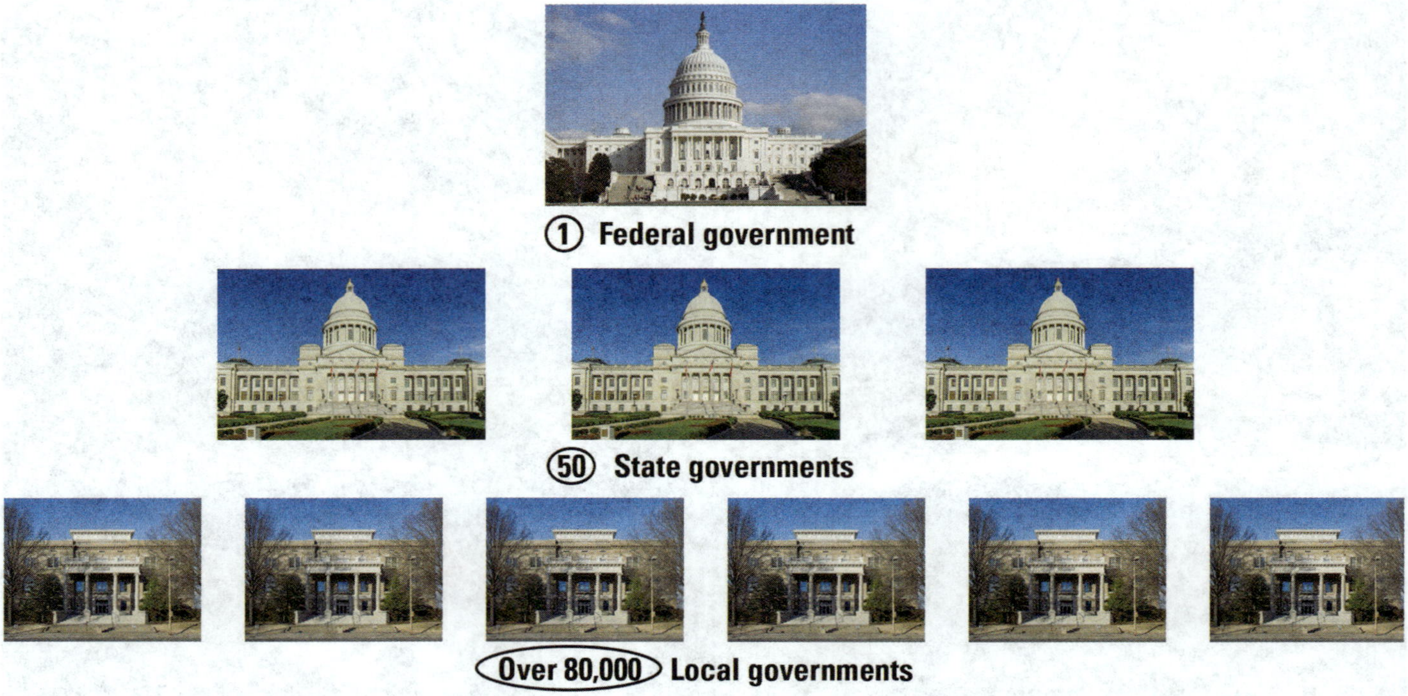

The United States has different levels of government. But all governments have to follow the Constitution.

3. Federal Government

People in each state have to follow their state's laws. But they also have to follow the laws of the U.S. government.

The U.S. government is called the **federal government**. It makes laws for the whole country. The basic rules of this government are set by the United States **Constitution**. States cannot disobey the Constitution.

The Constitution sets up how the federal government is structured. The government has a president, a legislature, and a court system.

People elect the president. The president leads the country and carries out laws.

People also elect leaders to Congress, which is the federal government's legislature. Congress makes laws for the United States.

The people elected President Biden to lead the country and carry out laws.

The highest court in the United States is called the Supreme Court. This court says what federal laws mean.

Like local and state governments, the federal government also provides public services. These services are available to everyone in the country. People pay taxes to the U.S. government so that it can provide services and protect the nation.

Have you sent mail at the post office or traveled on an interstate highway? If you have, then you have used services provided by the federal government. The military and public broadcasting are some other services the federal government provides.

The postal service is provided by the federal government.

4. Tribal Government

Tribal councils provide important services for the community, such as community gatherings. Here, tribal members from different tribes gather to celebrate community.

More than 5 million Native Americans live in the United States. Many Native Americans live on reservations. A reservation is land that is set aside by the federal government for tribal use. Reservations are run by a **tribal government**. There are more than 500 tribal governments in the United States.

Tribal governments have a special relationship with federal and state governments. Most tribal governments have a constitution. This means they are able to make their own laws. Tribes talk to the state and federal governments to ensure that their constitutions work together. Some tribes have governments similar to the federal government. A few tribes have a legislature and court system.

Tribal constitutions allow for the creation of tribal councils. The tribal council has the right to make laws that govern the tribe. It also makes important decisions. Tribal councils create their own police force, court system, and fire department. They also provide important services for the community, such as education, performances, and community gatherings.

There are many important issues that affect both tribal governments and other governments. In these cases, the tribal government and local government must work together. For example, both governments work together to protect the environment. When there is a fire that is quickly spreading, both governments will send crews to put the fire out. Tribal governments may also work with state and federal governments to prevent crimes or help the economy.

Tribal governments create their own fire departments. Pictured here is the Sycuan Golden Eagles Hotshot Crew, part of the Kumeyaay nation located in southern California.

Hands-On Activity Notes

Activity Online

Complete each step to create a podcast about governments.

Set Up Your Podcast

Some podcast ideas: ______________________________

____

____

Who is my audience? ______________________________

____

What is the main idea of my podcast? ______________________________

____

____

Who could I interview for the podcast? ______________________________

____

Plan What to Ask

Plan to ask at least three questions when you interview someone. Make sure to ask them for their opinion on a topic.

____

____

____

____

Plan What to Say

Plan the title of your podcast and what you will say in it. Remember to plan a beginning, middle, and end as you share good information on your topic.

Title:

Summary

There are different levels of government. Your community has its own government. So does your state and the country. Tribal governments work with state and federal governments to make laws to govern Native American tribes.

Each level of government provides services and makes laws. Taxes help fund the work of the government. The government's job is to help your community, state, and country run smoothly. People have a say in their government. How can you have a voice in your government? You'll learn that in our next lesson.

Show What You Know

List four different levels of government. Draw and describe one thing about each.

Lesson 15

Citizenship and Participation

How do we have a voice in our community?

Introduction

Has your family ever talked about how to spend a weekend or a vacation? Did you get to say what you thought? If so, then you probably felt better about the choice your family made. If not, then your family may have made a decision that you didn't like. Even if we don't get exactly what we want, we all like to have a voice in the decisions that affect us.

The same is true in your town or city. People want to have a voice in the decisions that affect their lives. Many people want to make their voices heard in state and federal governments, as well. They can make their voices heard in many ways, such as voting or attending public meetings. Also, helping to make important decisions in the community is part of being a good citizen. In this lesson, you'll learn about ways to make your voice heard in your community.

Vocabulary

ballot
candidate
civil rights
demonstration
peaceful
register
republic

People can make their voices heard in many ways. This image shows a demonstration in front of the Capitol building in Washington, D.C.

Preview Activity

Activity Online

Think of a time when your voice was heard and a time you felt your voice wasn't heard on a decision that affected you.

	When My Voice Was Heard	When My Voice Was Not Heard
What was the situation and the decision that was made?		
Did you agree with the decision?		
How did you feel?		
Draw a face in the box to show your feelings.		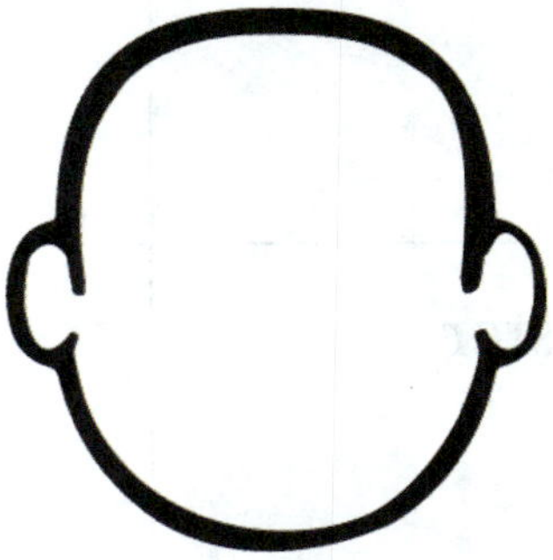

How important is it to you to have a voice in decisions that affect you? Vote below by placing a checkmark in one of the boxes:

❒ **Not Important** ❒ **Important** ❒ **Very Important**

Vocabulary Activity

Activity Online

Define each term. Describe what it might look or sound like. An example has been done for you.

Term	Definition	What It Might Look or Sound Like
ballot	A form on which people mark their votes in an election	People marking a piece of paper to vote
candidate		
civil rights		
demonstration		
peaceful		
register		
republic		

Hands-On Activity

Complete an infographic that explains the relationship between people and leaders in a republic. Explore the responsibilities of citizenship by taking part in a simulation of the democratic process.

Directions: Responsibilities in a Republic

1. **Read Section 1.** Learn how people and leaders play important roles in a republic.
2. **Use the descriptions in the boxes to complete an infographic.** The infographic explains the role of people and leaders in a republic.

Directions: Being a Good Citizen

1. **Analyze an image, then read Section 2.** Learn about one way you can have your voice heard in your community.
2. **Complete the Activity Notes for Section 2.** Show what you learned about the activity.
3. **Be ready to participate in the activity.** You will have a chance to experience the responsibilities of being a good citizen.
4. **Repeat Steps 1–3 for Sections 3–5.**

In order to win, this man must get support from the people that he would represent.

1. People Choose Our Leaders

You know that the United States has a government. But how does that government work?

The United States government is a **republic**. In a republic, the people choose leaders to make decisions for the country. The leaders are chosen in a democratic way. This means that citizens vote for their leaders.

Our government's power comes from the citizens. Citizens have a say in who makes decisions in our government. They consent, or agree, to let leaders run the country.

When members of government are chosen, they represent the people who elected them to office. They may have told these people what they planned to do. Now, they have a responsibility to keep their promises. Most importantly, they must do what is best for the people they represent.

The members of the government aren't the only people who have responsibilities. All citizens have responsibilities, especially those who can vote. U.S. citizens who are at least 18 years old have the right to vote.

The United States relies on its citizens to vote for the leaders of the country. It is important that voters stay informed on the issues so that they can choose a good person to represent them.

One of the best ways to stay informed is by reading the news. The news gives people important information. However, sometimes newspapers want you to vote for certain people. It is best to read different newspapers so you can make the best decision for yourself.

Voting gives people a chance to make changes. You might not always like laws that are made, but new leaders are chosen every few years. You can choose to vote for someone new who agrees with you.

Reading the news is a great way to stay informed about the issues in our country.

Hands-On Activity Notes

Activity Online

Complete the infographic. In the red boxes, put the terms from the Red Bank in the correct order to reveal a statement. In the blue boxes, match the responsibilities listed in the Blue Bank to the correct group: leaders or citizens. Use each term or phrase only once.

Red Bank

- ❒ Elect
- ❒ People
- ❒ Leaders

Blue Bank

- ❒ Keep promises
- ❒ Stay informed
- ❒ Represent the people
- ❒ Vote if they are 18+
- ❒ Choose good people

This is a public meeting in New York City.

2. Going to Public Meetings

One way to have a voice in your community is to go to public meetings. Towns and cities have meetings to talk about important decisions. These decisions affect everyone who lives in the community.

Before making decisions, leaders want to know what people think. They ask people to come to public meetings to share their thoughts and ideas. For instance, leaders might call a meeting to talk about traffic safety near schools. The leaders might ask whether the city should put speed bumps on certain streets to slow cars down.

Anyone can go to a public meeting. You can go just to listen or to share your thoughts on a topic.

If you choose to speak at a public meeting, then the leaders of the meeting may ask you questions. When you are finished, the next person gets to speak.

It can be hard to talk in front of a group. But if you are brave enough, then speaking at a public meeting will give you a voice in your community. You can tell the leaders of your town or city what you think. You can tell your neighbors, too. You might even change people's minds!

Speakers at a public meeting take turns sharing their thoughts.

3. Taking Part in Peaceful Demonstrations

Have you ever seen a **demonstration**? At a demonstration, people gather to show how they feel about an issue. A **peaceful** demonstration can be a good way of making your voice heard. Peaceful means not hurting others or their property.

Peaceful demonstrations let others know about a problem. People carry signs to show how they feel and listen to speeches. They may chant slogans, sing songs, or march in a parade.

In the 1950s and 1960s, there were many demonstrations in the United States about **civil rights**. Civil rights are rights that people have simply because they are citizens. For instance, all adult citizens have the right to vote.

These people are part of a peaceful demonstration.

This civil rights protest in Washington, D.C., took place in 1963.

Why were civil rights a problem in the 1950s and 1960s? At that time, many African Americans were not being given all their rights. For example, in some states, laws made it hard for them to vote.

Many people wanted these laws to change. Thousands of them took part in civil rights marches. These peaceful demonstrations made many Americans think more about civil rights. In time, new laws were passed to help give all citizens their rights.

Barack Obama was the first Black president of the United States. Here, he gives a speech to voters who support him.

4. Supporting a Candidate

Candidates are people who run for office. This means they try to get elected to do a certain job in government for the community. For example, several people may want the job of mayor. To run for this office, they become candidates.

People want to vote for candidates who will make their community a better place. So, candidates tell people about their ideas. They give speeches and talk to news reporters. They meet voters in public places, such as shopping malls. Sometimes they even visit people's homes. Then, voters choose the candidate they like best.

Candidates need lots of help. They can't talk to every voter. They need people to tell friends and neighbors about their ideas. They need money to send voters mail and to pay for ads on television and radio.

If you like a candidate's ideas, then you can help the person get elected. This is another way to have a voice in your community.

There are many ways to support a candidate. You can give money. You can put signs in your windows or in your yard. You can talk to voters. You can help mail letters to voters. On Election Day, you can encourage people to vote.

Supporting a candidate is one way to make your voice heard.

5. Voting

Voting is one of the best ways to have a voice in your community. People vote in elections to choose community leaders. They also can vote on ideas for improving their town or city.

When the United States was created, only certain people could vote. A voter had to be a White man who owned land. Over time, more and more people won the right to vote.

There are still a few rules about who can vote. Voters must be at least 18 years old and citizens of the United States. They also must **register,** or sign up, to vote.

People vote by marking a **ballot**. The ballot lists all the candidates and ideas to vote on. After everyone has voted, the ballots are counted to see which candidates and ideas have won.

People must register before they can vote.

These people are voting on Election Day.

Today, some people vote by mail. But most people vote in person on Election Day. They mark their ballots in small booths. The booths keep other people from seeing how they are voting.

Leaders make most of the decisions for a community. But in an election, every voter helps to choose ideas and candidates. In this way, voting gives people a strong voice in their community.

Hands-On Activity Notes

Activity Online

Complete each section after participating in each experience.

Section 2

Going to a public meeting gives people a voice in their community because ______________________________

____

Write what you would say at a public meeting.

____

____

____

____

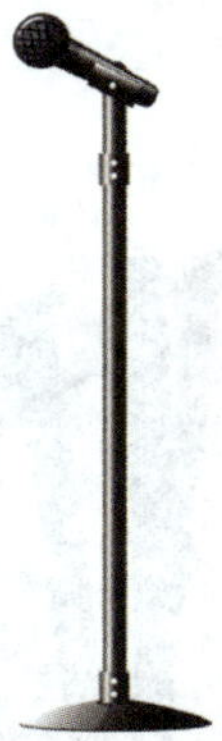

Section 3

Taking part in a peaceful demonstration gives people a voice in their community because ______________________________

____

____

Write something on the sign showing your support of either a STEM club or a sports club:

Section 4

Supporting a candidate gives people a voice in their community because ______________________________

____

____

Read each mayoral candidate's speech. Circle the argument that you most agree with.

Section 5

Voting gives people a voice in their community because

____

____

Cut out this voting card.

OFFICIAL MAYOR ELECTION BALLOT

Fill in one bubble only. Fold the ballot for secrecy when you are done.

Michael Thompson ◯

Fold along this line.

Sangita Reddy ◯

Cut out the ballot below when
you are ready to fill it out.

Your signature

Summary

The United States government is a republic, which means the people can choose their leaders. These leaders represent the people who elected them and make decisions that are best for the people they represent. U.S. citizens who are at least 18 years old can vote.

You can have a voice in your community in many ways. You can learn about issues and tell your opinions about them. You can attend public meetings. You also can take part in peaceful demonstrations. You can support and help candidates running for a government office.

Show What You Know

What are three issues in your community?

1. ______________________________
____
____

2. ______________________________
____
____

3. ______________________________
____
____

Design a poster that you could use at a peaceful demonstration for one of the issues.

Lesson 16
Making a Difference in the World

How can we help the world around us?

Introduction

We are all part of many communities. Some communities are small, like your school. Others are much bigger, like your state and country. The largest community of all is the global community. Everyone on Earth is a member of this community, and so are animals and other living things. We all share our planet's water, air, and soil. We all depend on each other to have healthy and happy lives.

It's up to us to take care of the planet. Sometimes humans hurt the environment with their actions, but there are many ways you can help out. This lesson has lots of ideas for ways to share our Earth. We can help both the people and environment around us. How many more ways to help can you think of?

Vocabulary

habitat

inclusive

These people are making a difference by carrying signs with slogans for causes they care about.

Preview Activity

Activity Online

After watching the video, answer the questions below.

Come up with a slogan that the group in the video might use.

___

___

___

What are some other ways you can make a difference in the world?

___

___

___

___

Vocabulary Activity

Activity Online

Write the definition in your own words. Then come up with a simple slogan and image to represent it.

Example:

community: A place where people live, work, and play

COMMUNITY

We all share a neighborhood

habitat:

inclusive:

Hands-On Activity

Examine bumper stickers to learn about actions you can take to make a difference in the world. Then plan and carry out a community service project.

Directions: Matching Bumper Sticker Slogans

1. **With a partner, examine an Activity Card.** Each contains a bumper sticker.
2. **Connect each bumper sticker to a section of your text.** What cause does the bumper sticker support?
3. **Complete a row in your Activity Notes.**
4. **Repeat Steps 1–3 until you have filled in all the rows in your Activity Notes.**

Directions: Community Service Project

1. **Read Section 9.** Learn about changes that can help improve the world.
2. **Complete your Activity Notes.** With your group, follow the stages of the inquiry process as outlined in your Activity Notes:
   - Identify a Problem
   - Ask Questions and Research
   - Provide Solutions
   - Develop an Action Plan
   - Prepare a Slogan and Pitch

1. Help Fight Air Pollution

You've seen how some people have tried to protect the environment. Let's look at some ways you can help.

One way to protect the environment is to fight air pollution. Cars are a major source of air pollution. So, you can help reduce air pollution by cutting down on how much you ride in cars.

Often, there are other ways to get where you want to go. Instead of riding in a car, you might be able to take a bus, a train, or a subway. Maybe you could ride a bike or walk.

Do you still need a car to get where you are going? Try to find other people who are going to the same place. Then, you can ride together in one car.

Biking, instead of using cars, helps fight air pollution.

2. Make Less Waste

A second way to help protect the environment is to make less waste. Most of our garbage goes into dumps called landfills. Many people worry that the waste in landfills can harm our air, soil, and water. Some places are running out of room to build new landfills.

How can you make less waste? Keep in mind the three R's: reduce, reuse, and recycle.

Reduce means to use less of things that will make waste. For example, your family can make less cardboard waste by buying one large box of cereal instead of several small ones. Your family can reduce toxic waste, too. When you buy products such as household cleaners, look for ones that don't have toxic chemicals in them.

Is there a recycling program where you live?

Reuse means to use things more than once. Use both sides of a sheet of paper before you recycle it. Try making arts and crafts from materials instead of throwing them away.

Recycle means to save waste so it can be used again to make new products. In many places, you can recycle cans, bottles, newspapers, and other materials.

3. Help Save Energy and Water

How many ways can you think of to save water?

A third way to help protect the environment is to save precious resources. Two of these resources are energy and water.

Remember, nonrenewable sources of energy cannot be replaced in a short time. And even fresh water may become scarce.

You can help by using energy wisely. Turn off lights when you leave a room. Turn off televisions and computers when no one is using them. In cold weather, put on a sweater instead of turning up the heat.

Use water wisely, too. Take shorter showers, and don't leave the water running when you brush your teeth. If you have a hose, use a nozzle you can turn off when you lay the hose down. Tell your school or city about sprinklers that are broken or that are watering the sidewalk instead of grass and plants.

4. Help Keep Animals Safe

We share the planet with many kinds of wildlife. Birds and other animals need our help to survive. Here are three ways that people can help keep animals safe—even animals that live far away from you.

What can you do to protect these animals?

First, buy food that has been caught or raised safely. For example, some nets used to catch tuna also trap and kill dolphins. But other nets are designed to allow dolphins to escape. Your family can help save dolphins by knowing what brands of tuna keep dolphins safe.

Second, don't buy products made from endangered animals. Some examples are coats made from fur, decorations made with ivory from elephants, and belts made of crocodile skins. Not buying these can keep animals safe.

Third, find out about dangers to wildlife in your area. For example, some chemicals used on grass and other plants can poison birds. If you have a garden or yard, learn how to make it a safer place for wildlife.

5. Help Save Animal Habitats

Picking up litter is one way to help wildlife.

You also can help animals by saving their **habitats**. Habitats are places where particular animals live, such as the forest or the seashore.

We often spoil animal habitats with our trash. Drinks are sometimes sold with plastic rings that hold bottles or cans together. Birds and other animals can get tangled in these rings. Animals can also choke on old balloons and other litter. Plastic bags that get washed into the ocean can harm fish and birds. So, don't be a litterbug! Even better, take along a trash bag when you go to a park or a beach, and pick up any litter you find.

You also can support groups that work to save animal habitats around the world. You can find many of these groups on the Internet. Some groups even have kids' clubs you can join.

6. Share with Other People

People in friendly communities help one another. Nearly all of us can do something to help others in our global community.

One way to help is by sharing the things we have. If you have old clothes, don't throw them away. Maybe someone else in your family can use the clothes you've outgrown. Or, you can give them to groups that collect clothes for people in need.

Other groups collect food or toys for families who can't afford to buy them. You may have seen collection barrels at your supermarket or school. Don't pass them by! You might have canned food in your kitchen that your family can give away. Or you might be able to save up to buy a toy or some food. Even one can of food can be a big help to someone.

Do you have food drives where you live?

UNICEF sends help to children around the world.

7. Lend a Helping Hand

Many groups bring people together to lend others a helping hand. You can help others by joining a group that's right for you.

One such group might be UNICEF (pronounced YOO-nih-sehf). UNICEF helps needy children around the world. Every Halloween, thousands of kids in the United States trick-or-treat to collect money for UNICEF instead of candy for themselves.

One town in California has a group of children who raise money to help youth in need around the world. They provide books, help fund treatment for the sick, and even have a scholarship for children interested in the arts. If you can't find a group to join, then maybe you can start one.

8. Treat Others with Respect

Everyone needs respect. You can make a big difference by being **inclusive**. Being inclusive means that you include every type of person, even if they are different from you.

It's hurtful to make fun of others or to harm them because of how they look, dress, or talk. Act kindly instead. If you see people who are not being inclusive of others, then speak up. Remind them that everyone deserves respect.

Take time to learn about other people. The more you know about others, the more you will respect them. Talk to new people in your school or town. You might even try becoming pen pals with a child in another country.

No matter how someone looks or acts, you should treat them with respect.

Hands-On Activity Notes

Activity Online

Complete the correct row after examining an Activity Card.

Bumper Sticker	Section Number	Description of the Problem and One Thing I Can Do

Bumper Sticker	Section Number	Description of the Problem and One Thing I Can Do

9. Help Make Changes to Improve the World

How can you start helping the world? First, find a problem that interests you. It may be one from this lesson or something very different.

Asking questions about the problem is a great way to start. Ask questions like: what is causing the problem? And what is being done to stop it? If you were interested in protecting wildlife, you might ask: how are humans putting some animals in danger? And why is it important to help these animals? Think of other questions you can ask.

There are many places to look for answers to these questions. Websites online are a great source of information on the internet. Be careful, though, because not everything you see online is true. Some websites might be written by someone who is not informed on the issues.

Books and magazines are helpful, too. Like websites, some are more reliable than others. You also can ask adults who may know more, like your parents or teacher.

The internet is a good place to start finding information.

Keep an open mind when finding answers. People have many opinions, so different sources may give you different answers. Pay attention to who is providing the information. Look for evidence that supports the answer. Your job is to decide which answer is best.

Now, it is time to use what you know. You can gather other students who also want to protect animals. People are more likely to listen to a large group than a small group.

There are many ways to make change. You can try to spread the message about the problem to others. You could put up signs telling people how they can help wildlife. You can try to raise money for the cause.

You even can talk to people in the government. They could pass a law that helps animals. This is hard to do, but it is one of the greatest changes you can make.

To make a change, you can inform other people about the problem.

Hands-On Activity Notes

Complete each step to plan your community service project.

Activity Online

Identify a Problem

What is a problem that you are interested in helping to solve?

___

___

___

___

Ask Questions and Research

My questions are . . .

___

___

___

___

Here is what I found as answers to my questions . . .

___

___

___

Sources:

___

Provide Solutions

Possible solutions are . . .

Sources:

Develop an Action Plan

Steps that need to be completed for this project (list at least four):

1.

2.

3.

4.

List of materials or needs for the project:

Prepare a Slogan

My ideas for a slogan are . . .

Summary

We are all members of the global community. There are things you can do to take care of the planet. You can help protect the environment, share things with other people, and get involved with organizations that help others.

There are many problems that you can help solve. You can choose a topic that interests you. You can ask questions about the topic and look for answers to the questions. You can try to make a difference in the world!

Show What You Know

Identify one problem related to each of the topics below. Then explain at least one specific action you could take as a solution.

Helping the Environment 	Problem:	Solution:
Helping Wildlife 	Problem:	Solution:
Helping People 	Problem:	Solution:

World Political Map

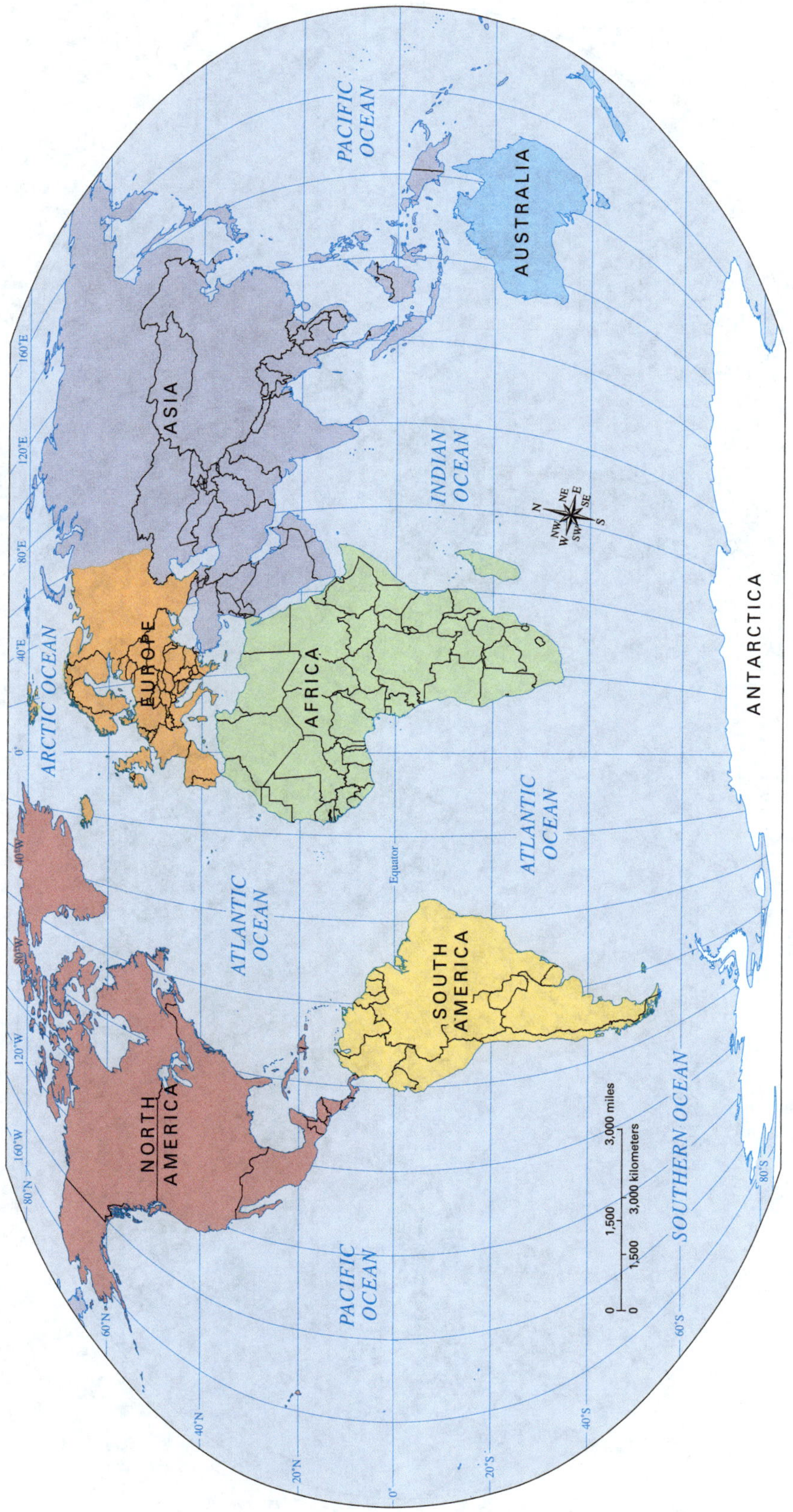

World Physical Map

United States Political Map

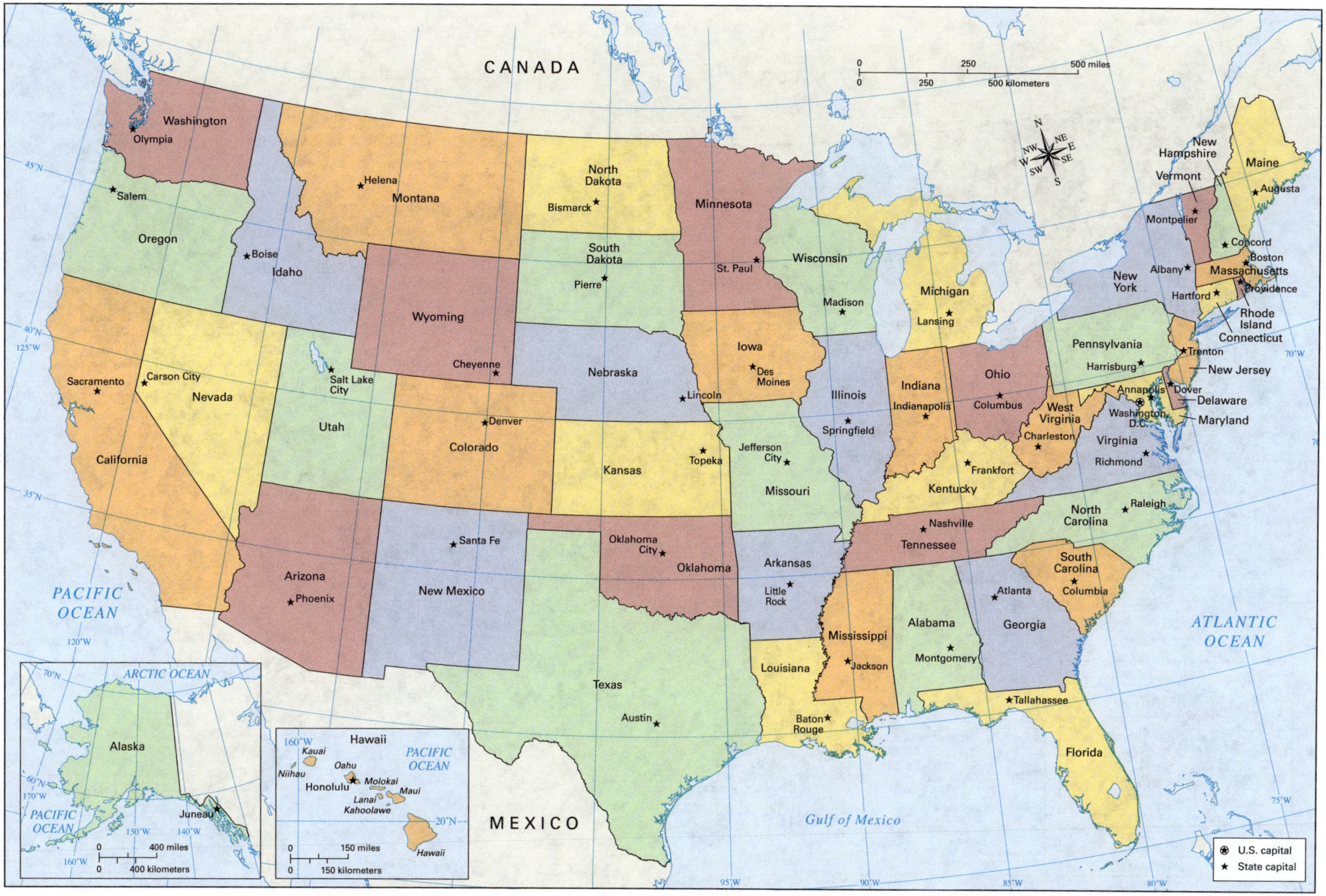

United States Physical Map

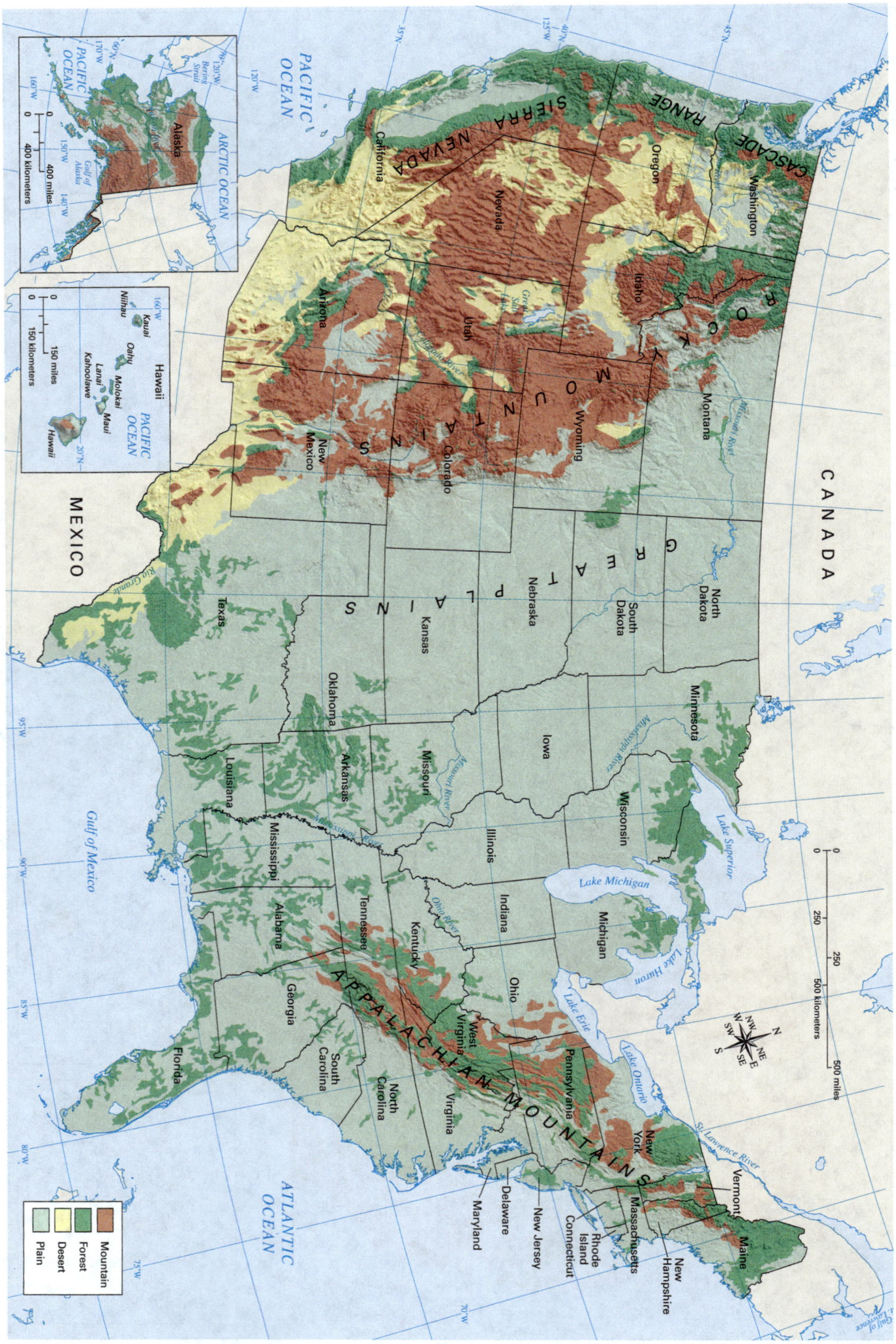

A

adapt to change ways of living to fit an environment

B

ballot a form on which people mark their votes in an election

border the line where one place, such as a state or country, ends and another begins

boycott when people refuse to buy products from a certain business

C

canal a waterway made by humans

candidate a person who tries to get elected to do a job in government for a community

canyon a deep, narrow valley with steep sides

capital the city where the government of a country or state meets

cardinal direction one of the four main directions: north, east, south, and west

citizen a person who is born in a country or who chooses to become a member of that country by law

citizenship the rights and responsibilities of citizens

city hall the building where the offices of a community's government are located

civil rights rights a person has as a citizen

climate the weather in a place, measured over time

common good the things that are good for everyone in a community

compelling question a question you just need to know the answer to

conservation the careful use of natural resources

Constitution the document that sets up the basic rules of the United States government

continent one of the seven large bodies of land on Earth

country an area of land that has its own government

culture a way of life shared by a group of people

D

demand the total amount of a good or service that customers will buy at all prices

demonstration a gathering of people to show shared feelings or opinions

disabled not being able to do an everyday thing, such as walk, in the same way that most people can

discriminate to treat people unfairly because they belong to a different group

diverse made up of different groups of people and cultures

E

economy the system in which goods and services are bought and sold

evidence the facts you use to back up your claim

environment Earth's air, water, soil, and living things

equator the imaginary line that divides Earth into the Northern and Southern hemispheres

F

fact a true piece of information

federal government the national government of the United States

first responder a person trained to give help at the scene of an emergency

free market economy an economy where choices are left up to each buyer and seller

G

geography the study of Earth—its spaces, land, water, air, and people

global trade the buying and selling of goods and services between countries around the world

goods items that can be bought, sold, and traded, such as food and computers

government a group that helps run a community, state, or country

H

habitat a place where particular animals live

I

inclusive including every type of person, even if they are different from you

immigrant a person who comes from another place to live in a country

incentive something that leads a person to make a certain choice

interest extra money that you make from saving money at a bank

invest using money in the hopes of making more money in the future

L

legislature the part of the government that makes laws

local government the government of a city, town, county, or other area in the United States that is smaller than a state

M

map key a feature that explains what the symbols on a map stand for

manufactured made with machines

market a place where buyers and sellers come together

N

natural hazard a force of nature that shapes Earth

natural resource a useful item that comes from nature, such as wood from trees

O

ocean one of the five largest bodies of water on Earth

opinion what someone thinks or believes

P

peaceful done without hurting others or their property

physical feature a natural feature of Earth's surface, such as a mountain, plain, lake, or river

physical geography the physical features, climate, and natural resources of a place

primary source an object created by someone who was at an event

prime meridian the imaginary line that divides Earth into the Eastern and Western hemispheres

private service a service that is provided for money by a business

profit the amount of money earned by a business after costs are removed

pollution anything that makes air, water, or soil dirty or unsafe

public service a service, such as a public library, that is offered by a community to everyone

public works things such as roads, water pipes, and streetlights that everyone in a community uses

R

region an area with certain common features that set it apart from other areas

register to sign up to vote

republic a type of government in which the citizens elect their leaders to represent them

S

scale a feature used to figure out distances on a map

scarcity when people want more things than they can actually have

services tasks you pay someone to do for you

state one of the 50 main areas with their own governments that make up the United States

state government the government of one of the states of the United States

strike when workers stop working to try to get something they want, such as better pay

suburb a community that grows up on the edge of a city

supply the total amount of a good or service available to buy

symbol an object that stands for something else (for example, the Liberty Bell is a symbol of freedom)

T

tax money that people pay to a government

tribal government a government that interacts with the federal government as a sovereign nation and has legal jurisdiction over its own land

CREDITS

Cover and Title Page
Tetra Images / Alamy Stock Photo

Frontmatter
viBL: Lorelyn Medina / Adobe Stock

Unit 1 Opener
1: Shutterstock

Lesson 1
7: NASA **9:** Shutterstock **11:** alexlmx / Adobe Stock Photo **11:** Ina / Adobe Stock Photo **12:** robert / Adobe Stock Images **15:** Getty Images **16:** Shutterstock **18:** NASA **20T:** ihba / Adobe Stock Images **20B:** Ilene MacDonald/ Alamy **21B:** Ilene MacDonald/ Alamy **25T:** Shutterstock **25B:** Fotosearch.com **30:** Fotosearch.com

Lesson 2
31: iofoto / Adobe Stock Images **35:** Samuel B. / Adobe Stock Photo **36:** Pixabay **37:** LianeM / Adobe Stock Images **38L:** moodboard / Adobe Stock Images **38R:** Shutterstock **39:** Robert Marmion/Alamy **42:** Shutterstock **43:** Getty Images **44:** rabbit75_fot / Adobe Stock Images **45:** Getty Images **46:** kojihirano / Adobe Stock Images **47:** Dreamstime **48 B:** Aquarius / Adobe Stock Photo **50:** Fotosearch.com

Lesson 3
51: Bambi L. Dingman / Dreamstime **55:** Wave Break Media Ltd | Dreamstime.com **57:** Shutterbas | Dreamstime.com **62:** Jmaentz / Dreamstime **63:** Leigh Prather / Dreamstime **64:** Kitty Miller **65:** Grecaud Paul / Adobe Stock Image **66:** iStockphoto **67:** Neutronman / Dreamstime **68:** Shutterstock **69:** Matt Campbell-epa / Corbis **70:** Getty Images **71:** Wikimedia

Lesson 4
75: Howard Sandler | Dreamstime.com **77:** Map Resources / Adobe Stock Images **78:** Library of Congress **79:** Oksana Kumer / Adobe Stock Images **79:** Pixel-Shot / Adobe Stock Images **79:** Jelena Ivanovic / Adobe Stock Images **79:** James M. Davidson / Adobe Stock Images **80T:** Shutterstock **81T:** Susan Vineyard | Dreamstime.com **82T:** Pat Canova / Alamy Stock Photo **83T:** Ivo Roospold / Alamy Stock Photo **84T:** John Wollwerth | Dreamstime.com **85T:** Nancy G Western Photography, Nancy Greifenhagen / Alamy Stock Photo **86:** Library of Congress **87:** Pierre Jean Durieu | Dreamstime.com **88T:** kellyvandellen / Adobe Stock Images **88B:** traveller70 / Adobe Stock Images **89T:** rceron69 / Adobe Stock Images **89B:** Wikipedia **90B:** Tom / Adobe Stock Images **91BC:** Wikipedia **91TC:** Danita Delimont / Alamy Stock Photo **91BL:** Wikimedia **91BR:** Wikimedia **91TL:** Wikipedia **91TR:** Library of Congress **91:** Shutterstock

Unit 2 Opener
93: Pixabay

Lesson 5
99: Library of Congress **101L:** Linda Harms / Alamy Stock Photo **101R:** iStockphoto **106:** Library of Congress **107:** Library of Congress **108:** Library of Congress **109:** Library of Congress **110:** Library of Congress **111:** Shutterstock **112:** iStockphoto **113L:** Library of Congress **113R:** Wikimedia **114:** iStockphoto **115:** Ivy Close Images/Alamy

Lesson 6
119: blickwinkel/Alamy **121TL:** MacroOne / Adobe Stock Images **121TC:** zaurrahimov / Adobe Stock Images **121TR:** antto / Adobe Stock Images **121CR:** davooda / Adobe Stock Images **123:** drubig-photo / Adobe Stock Images **124:** Library of Congress **125:** MBI/Alamy **128B:** dbimages/Alamy **128T:** Ufuk Uyanik/Dreamstime **129:** Pierre Arsenault/Alamy **130:** iStockphoto **131:** Richard Levine/age fotostock / Superstock **132:** Richard Gunion/ Dreamstime **133:** Purestock/Alamy **134:** Sergio Vila/Dreamstime **135:** Radius Images/Alamy **136:** Corbis **137:** Sbukley/Dreamstime

Lesson 7
141: Thinkstock **143:** iStockphoto **144:** Getty Images **145T:** Raymond Gehman/Corbis **145B:** Andrey Kuzmin / Adobe Stock Images **147:** JackF / Adobe Stock Images **148:** Library of Congress **149:** Shutterstock **150:** Library of Congress **151:** Getty Images **152:** Getty Images **153:** iStockphoto **154:** Corbis **155:** Corbis **156:** ZUMA Press, Inc. / Alamy Stock Photo **157:** Purestock / Alamy Stock Photo **158:** ASSOCIATE PRESS **159:** Shutterstock **162T:** Suesse / Adobe Stock Images **162TC:** antto / Adobe Stock Images **162BC:** blankstock / Adobe Stock Images **162B:** dstarky / Adobe Stock Images

Lesson 8

169: Corbis **171:** Shutterstock **172:** Danita Delimont/Alamy **173:** venimo / Adobe Stock Images **175:** Painterstock / Adobe Stock Images **175:** zzzdim / Adobe Stock Images **176T:** Corbis **177:** Getty Images **178TL:** ton koene / Alamy Stock Photo **178TC:** Wikimedia **178B:** Shutterstock **178C:** Shutterstock **179B:** Courtesy of Charles Shafsky **181TL:** J.Enrique Molina / Alamy Stock Photo **181TC:** Wikimedia **181C:** Shutterstock **181B:** Shutterstock **182T:** Kobackpacko | Dreamstime.com **182B:** Sai0112 | Dreamstime.com **183B:** liubovyashkir / Adobe Stock Images **184TL:** Moshe Einhorn / Alamy Stock Photo **184TC:** Wikimedia **184C:** Shutterstock **184B:** Shutterstock **185B:** Getty Images **186:** Shutterstock **187TL:** Shutterstock **187TC:** Wikimedia **187C:** Shutterstock **187B:** Shutterstock **188T:** Damian Tully/Alamy **189:** badescu / Adobe Stock Images **190TL:** Shutterstock **190TC:** Wikimedia **190C:** Shutterstock **190B:** Shutterstock **191B:** powderkeg stock/Alamy **192:** Corbis **193TL:** Shutterstock **193TC:** Wikimedia **193C:** Anton Ivanov / Alamy Stock Photo **193B:** Shutterstock

Unit 3 Opener

195: Getty Images

Lesson 9

201: iStockphoto **203:** Ruslan / Adobe Stock Images **204L:** mapo / Adobe Stock Images **204R:** mitrushova / Adobe Stock Images **205:** stockyimages / Adobe Stock Images **205:** Asier / Adobe Stock Images **205:** Tom Wang / Adobe Stock Images **205:** valiza14 / Adobe Stock Images **205:** pressmaster / Adobe Stock Images **206:** Getty Images **207:** DragonImages / Adobe Stock Images **208:** iStockphoto **209:** Yuko / Adobe Stock Images **210:** iStockphoto **211:** iStockphoto **212:** iStockphoto **213:** iStockphoto **214:** nyul / Adobe Stock Images **215:** silverkblack / Adobe Stock Images

Lesson 10

219: Thinkstock **223:** Nomad_Soul / Adobe Stock Images **223:** Gelpi / Adobe Stock Images **223:** Valua Vitaly / Adobe Stock Images **223:** Brastock / Adobe Stock Images **223:** khosrork / Adobe Stock Images **224:** michaeljung / Adobe Stock Images **225:** Thinkstock **226:** Rusty / Adobe Stock Images **227B:** Thinkstock **227T:** Thinkstock **228:** Thinkstock **231:** Pixel-Shot / Adobe Stock Images **234T:** iStockphoto **234B:** iStockphoto **235:** Judith Morrison / Adobe Stock Images

Lesson 11

237: iStockphoto **239:** Robert Byron | Dreamstime **240:** Monster Ztudio / Adobe Stock Images **241:** napatcha / Adobe Stock Images **241:** Ranta Images / Adobe Stock Images **241:** Yury Kisialiou / Adobe Stock Images **241:** duncanandison / Adobe Stock Images **242:** chrupka / Adobe Stock Images **243:** Getty Images **244:** Deyan Georgiev Authentic collection/Alamy **245:** chones / Adobe Stock Images **246:** Rawpixel.com / Adobe Stock Images **247:** Getty Images **248:** Pixel-Shot / Adobe Stock Images **249T:** Comaniciu Dan Dumitru/ Dreamstime **249B:** Anna Khomulo / Adobe Stock Images **250:** auremar / Adobe Stock Images **251:** Mihail / Adobe Stock Images **252T:** nadiinko / Adobe Stock Images **252C:** Rovshan / Adobe Stock Images **252B:** The Noun Project **253T:** The Noun Project **253C:** iconsv / Adobe Stock Images **253B:** Mykola / Adobe Stock Images **254:** Good Studio / Adobe Stock Images

Lesson 12

255: Getty Images **257:** Peter Hermes Furian / Adobe Stock **260L:** Shutterstock **260R:** Shutterstock **261:** Gary Blakeley / Adobe Stock Images **262:** Getty Images **263:** Curioso.Photography / Adobe Stock Images **264:** iStockphoto **265:** Pa2011/Dreamstime **266:** iStockphoto **267:** iStockphoto **268:** Getty Images **269:** Getty Images

Unit 4 Opener

273: Dragana Gordic / Adobe Stock Images

Lesson 13

279: Shutterstock **281TL:** Pixabay **281TC:** Pixabay **281TR:** Pixabay **281BL:** adragan / Adobe Stock Images **281BC:** Pixabay **281BR:** daria_serdtseva / Adobe Stock Images **282:** Pixabay **282:** Go Ahead / Adobe Stock Images **283:** JenkoAtaman / Adobe Stock Images **283:** Anatoliy Karlyuk / Adobe Stock Images **284:** Rmarmion/Dreamstime **285:** Robert Kneschke/Dreamstime **287:** iStockphoto **288:** iStockphoto **289:** Thinkstock **290L:** Rafael Ben-Ari/ Alamy **290R:** iStockphoto **291:** Irina Brinza/Dreamstime **292:** Steven Frame/Dreamstime **293:** iStockphoto **294:** Monkey Business Images/ Dreamstime **295:** Photodisc/Getty Images **296:** Wikimedia **297:** Ian Klein/ Dreamstime **298:** Image Source/Alamy **299T:** iStockphoto **299B:** iStockphoto **300:** Pixabay **300:** Pixabay **300:** Pixabay **300:** Pixabay **300:** Viacheslav Iakobchuk / Adobe Stock Images **300:** Pixabay **300:** Pixabay **300:** Monkey Business / Adobe Stock Images **300:** miriristic / Adobe Stock Images **300:** Pixabay **300:** Pixabay **300:** Pixabay **300:** Brad Pict / Adobe Stock Images **300:** Pixabay **300:** kuosumo / Adobe Stock Images **300:** Pixabay **300:** Pixabay **300:** Pixabay

Lesson 14

304: Steven Greaves/Corbis **305:** GAYSORN / Adobe Stock Images **305:** happyvector071 / Adobe Stock Images **307:** ngad / Adobe Stock Images **307:** fotomek / Adobe Stock Images **307:** Konstantin Yuganov / Adobe Stock Images **308:** iStockphoto **309:** Rmarmion/ Dreamstime **310:** Shutterstock **311:** Shutterstock **312T:** iStockphoto **312T:** Thinkstock **312T:** Shutterstock **312B:** Shutterstock **313:** iStockphoto **314:** Richard Broadwell / Alamy **315:** ZUMA Press, Inc. / Alamy

Lesson 15

319: Shutterstock **322TL:** Pixabay **323:** labalajadia / Adobe Stock Images **323:** Gelpi / Adobe Stock Images **323:** rosliothman / Adobe Stock Images **324:** 2/Ocean/Corbis **325:** Shutterstock **326L:** vector_s / Adobe Stock Images **327T:** iStockphoto **327B:** Thinkstock **328:** Shutterstock **329:** Library of Congress **330:** iStockphoto **331:** Shutterstock **332:** Jonathan Nourok/Getty Images **333:** Blend Images/Alamy **334B:** creativeteam / Adobe Stock Images **335L:** jenny on the moon / Adobe Stock Images **335R:** jenny on the moon / Adobe Stock Images **337:** Pixabay

Lesson 16

339: Shutterstock **341:** Monkey Business / Adobe Stock Images **343:** Carolyn Franks / Adobe Stock Images **343:** Samuel B. / Adobe Stock Images **343:** DG-Studio / Adobe Stock Images **344:** Stockbyte/Getty Images **345:** Diane Macdonald/Getty Images **346:** iStockphoto **347T:** Shutterstock **347C:** James Gritz/Getty Images **347B:** Jeremy Woodhouse/ Getty Images **348:** iStockphoto **349:** Thinkstock **350:** Horizons WWP/ Alamy **351:** SW Productions/Getty Images **354:** iStockphoto **355:** 2/Nick White/Ocean/Corbis **358T:** nirutft / Adobe Stock Images **358C:** Greg Brave / Adobe Stock Images **358B:** Goffkein / Adobe Stock Images